Series Editor:
Hans Kröger

Political Speeches

Historical & Topical Issues

Edited by
Wiltrud Frenken, Angela Luz
and Brigitte Prischtt

EINFACH ENGLISCH

Schöningh

Zu dieser Textausgabe ist eine Audio-CD mit ausgewählten Texten erhältlich. Sie kann über den Buchhandel oder direkt beim Schöningh Verlag bezogen werden:

- Political Speeches – Historical & Topical Issues
  Audio-CD, Best.-Nr. 062409-1

Sprachliche Betreuung: Simone Duxbury-Ziemer

www.schoeningh-schulbuch.de
Schöningh Verlag, Jühenplatz 1 – 3, 33098 Paderborn

Druck 5 4 3 2 1 / Jahr 2011 10 09 08 07
Die letzte Zahl bezeichnet das Jahr dieses Druckes.

Umschlaggestaltung: Peter Wypior, Bad Driburg; Foto: © picture-alliance/KPA/HIP/ Spectrum Colour Library
Druck und Bindung: westermann druck GmbH, Braunschweig

ISBN 978-3-14-041234-6

Contents

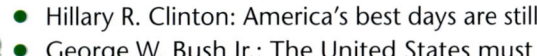

IV. Postcolonial times

V. Globalisation

Developing skills

Getting started

This collage shows pictures and people who have spoken in public about important issues.

1. Name the people you recognize and speak about them.
2. Speculate about what issues they might have given a speech on.

I. The power of words

 ### William Shakespeare: Marc Antony's funeral oration

This speech is taken from Shakespeare's *Julius Caesar*. Julius Caesar returns to Rome in 44 B. C., victorious from battle. The crowd in Rome is ecstatic, and they attempt to crown him King three times but he refuses. Some of the generals in his army become concerned about Caesar's power and his penchant for extreme and tyrannical actions. They believe they should kill him. The assassinators succeed in their plan, however, they are afraid that his followers could stir up the people of Rome. When Marc Antony enters the Senate a short time later, he is visibly upset about the deed, but avoids a direct confrontation and merely asks for the favour of giving a funeral oration for Caesar thereby paying him his last respects. The conspirators foresee the danger, but at Brutus's recommendation do not dare to refuse Marc Antony's request.

plebeian the common people of ancient Rome

public chair pulpit for orations

beholding indebted

blest blessed

countryman a person from one's own country; a compatriot

interrèd buried; placed in a grave

FIRST PLEBEIAN: Stay, ho! And let us hear Mark Antony.
THIRD PLEBEIAN: Let him go into the public chair;
  We'll hear him. Noble Antony, go up.
ANTONY: For Brutus' sake, I am beholding to you.
FOURTH PLEBEIAN: What does he say of Brutus? 5
THIRD PLEBEIAN: He says, for Brutus' sake
  He finds himself beholding to us all.
FOURTH PLEBEIAN: 'Twere best he speak no harm of Brutus here!
FIRST PLEBEIAN: This Caesar was a tyrant.
THIRD PLEBEIAN: Nay, that's certain. 10
  We are blest that Rome is rid of him.
SECOND PLEBEIAN: Peace! Let us hear what Antony can say.
ANTONY: You gentle Romans –
SECOND PLEBEIAN: Peace, ho! let us hear him.
ANTONY: Friends, Romans, countrymen, lend me your ears; 15
  I come to bury Caesar, not to praise him.
  The evil that men do lives after them,
  The good is oft interrèd with their bones;
  So let it be with Caesar. The noble Brutus
  Hath told you Caesar was ambitious. 20

If it were so, it was a grievous fault,
And grievously hath Caesar answered it.
Here, under leave of Brutus and the rest –
For Brutus is an honourable man;
5   So are they all, all honourable men –
Come I to speak in Caesar's funeral.
He was my friend, faithful and just to me;
But Brutus says he was ambitious,
And Brutus is an honourable man.
10   He hath brought many captives home to Rome,
Whose ransoms did the general coffers fill:
Did this in Caesar seem ambitious?
When that the poor have cried, Caesar hath wept;
Ambition should be made of sterner stuff:
15   Yet Brutus says he was ambitious,
And Brutus is an honourable man.
You all did see that on the Lupercal
I thrice presented him a kingly crown,
Which he did thrice refuse. Was this ambition?
20   Yet Brutus says he was ambitious,
And sure he is an honourable man.
I speak not to disprove what Brutus spoke,
But here I am to speak what I do know.
You all did love him once, not without cause;
25   What cause withholds you then to mourn for him?
O judgement! Thou art fled to brutish beasts,
And men have lost their reason. Bear with me;
My heart is in the coffin there with Caesar,
And I must pause till it come back to me.
30 FIRST PLEBEIAN: Methinks there is much reason in his sayings.
SECOND PLEBEIAN: If thou consider rightly of the matter,
Caesar has had great wrong.
THIRD PLEBEIAN: Has he, masters?
I fear there will a worse come in his place.
35 FOURTH PLEBEIAN: Marked ye his words? He would not take the
crown;
Therefore 'tis certain he was not ambitious.
FIRST PLEBEIAN: If it be found so, some will dear abide it.
SECOND PLEBEIAN: Poor soul! His eyes are red as fire with
40   weeping.
THIRD PLEBEIAN: There's not a nobler man in Rome than
                                        Antony.
FOURTH PLEBEIAN: Now mark him; he begins again to speak.
ANTONY: But yesterday the word of Caesar might
45   Have stood against the world; now lies he there,

grievous causing great pain or suffering

brought brought people, prisoners back with him to Rome
ransom money paid to get back a prisoner, slave or captured goods

Lupercal a grotto on the Palatine Hill in Rome sacred to Lupercus, the Lycean Pan

to withhold to hold back, to restrain

to bear with to be patient with

I fear there will a worse come in his place a common Elizabethan saying

dear abide it dearly pay the penalty for it

none ... reverence the lowest member of society considers it beneath him to pay his respects to Caesar
to stir to cause to feel strong emotions
mutiny disorder, riot
to wrong sb to treat sb in an unfair or incorrect manner

parchment *Pergament*. here: a written document
closet a small private room

napkin handkerchief; the reference is to the practice of keeping cloths stained in the blood of martyrs as relics
to bequeath to arrange to give money or property to others after your death
issue here: children or heirs

meet fitting, proper

to inflame to make sb's feelings of anger, passion, etc. much stronger

to stay to wait
o'ershot myself said more than I intended

villain a bad person or criminal

to descend to move from a higher level to a lower one

And none so poor to do him reverence.
O masters! If I were disposed to stir
Your hearts and minds to mutiny and rage
I should do Brutus wrong, and Cassius wrong,
Who, you all know, are honourable men.   5
I will not do them wrong; I rather choose
To wrong the dead, to wrong myself and you,
Than I will wrong such honourable men.
But here's a parchment with the seal of Caesar;
I found it in his closet; 'tis his will.   10
Let but the commons hear this testament,
Which, pardon me, I do not mean to read,
And they would go and kiss dead Caesar's wounds,
And dip their napkins in his sacred blood,
Yea, beg a hair of him for memory,   15
And, dying, mention it within their wills,
Bequeathing it as a rich legacy
Unto their issue.
FOURTH PLEBEIAN: We'll hear the will. Read it, Mark Antony.
ALL: The will, the will! We will hear Caesar's will!   20
ANTONY: Have patience, gentle friends; I must not read it.
    It is not meet you know how Caesar loved you.
    You are not wood, you are not stones, but men;
    And being men, hearing the will of Caesar,
    It will inflame you, it will make you mad.   25
    'Tis good you know not that you are his heirs;
    For if you should, O, what would come of it?
FOURTH PLEBEIAN: Read the will! We'll hear it, Antony!
    You shall read us the will, Caesar's will!
ANTONY: Will you be patient? Will you stay awhile?   30
    I have o'ershot myself to tell you of it.
    I fear I wrong the honourable men
    Whose daggers have stabbed Caesar; I do fear it.
FOURTH PLEBEIAN: They were traitors. Honourable men!
ALL: The will! The testament!   35
SECOND PLEBEIAN: They were villains, murderers! The will!
    Read the will!
ANTONY: You will compel me then to read the will?
    Then make a ring about the corpse of Caesar,
    And let me show you him that made the will.   40
    Shall I descend? And will you give me leave?
ALL: Come down.
    Antony comes down from the pulpit.

Abraham Lincoln: Gettysburg address (1863)

Abraham Lincoln was President from 1861–1865. Although Lincoln came from a state favouring slavery, he rejected it. In 1837, he was one of the delegates who protested against slavery in written form. After his election into the US-Congress in 1846, he developed a plan for the gradual emancipation of slaves in the District of Columbia. From 1856 on, Lincoln became involved with the newly-founded Republican Party. As a reaction to his election as President, seven southern states prepared their secession from the USA. Eventually this sparked off the War of Secession. Despite initial defeats, the northern states were able to claim victory in the end. Lincoln stands for the political virtues of the USA as he formulated during the Civil War on 19 November 1863 in his famous "Gettysburg Address", a short speech in the context of a commemorative service after the Battle of Gettysburg (Pennsylvania) in which both sides had respectively lost 25,000 men.

Fourscore and seven years ago our fathers brought forth on this continent a new nation, conceived in liberty and dedicated to the proposition that all men are created equal.

Now we are engaged in a great civil war, testing whether that
5 nation or any nation so conceived and so dedicated can long endure. We are met on a great battlefield of that war. We have come to dedicate a portion of that field as a final resting-place for those who here gave their lives that that nation might live. It is altogether fitting and proper that we should
10 do this.

But, in a larger sense, we cannot dedicate, we cannot consecrate, we cannot hallow this ground. The brave men, living and dead who struggled here have consecrated it far above our poor power to add or detract. The world will little note
15 nor long remember what we say here, but it can never forget what they did here. It is for us the living rather to be dedicated here to the unfinished work which they who fought here have thus far so nobly advanced. It is rather for us to be here dedicated to the great task remaining before us – that
20 from these honored dead we take increased devotion to that cause for which they gave the last full measure of devotion – that we here highly resolve that these dead shall not have died in vain, that this nation under God shall have a new birth of freedom, and that government of the people, by the
25 people, for the people shall not perish from the earth.

fourscore and seven years (4x20+7) = 87 years
to bring forth to bring into existence
to conceive to have the idea for
to dedicate to give oneself a specific cause
proposition a statement that affirms or denies sth

"all men are created equal" Lincoln quotes from the Declaration of Independence of the USA in 1776.

In the **American Civil War** (1861–1865) the "Union" fought against 11 southern states who had left the Union and confederated as the "Confederate States of America". The most important result of the bitterly fought war was the abolition of slavery.

to consecrate to render holy by means of religious rites
to hallow to treat or keep as sacred
to detract to take away from

to perish to disappear, die out

Winston Churchill: **Blood, toil, tears and sweat (1940)**

toil hard work, esp. that which is physically tiring

After the first 9 months of the Second World War, the Conservative government that had been led by Arthur Neville Chamberlain since 1937 had clearly lost parliamentary and public backing. The Prime Minister, discredited by his strong adherence to an appeasement policy towards Hitler and criticized for the lack of successes in the first months of war, found himself confronted with a vote virtually equivalent to a vote of no confidence on 8th May 1940. Against the background of the quick German invasions into the Netherlands, Belgium and Norway, Winston Churchill (1874–1965) was thereupon offered on 10th May the command of an all-party war coalition that was also to be supported by the two formerly opposition parties (Labour and Liberals). When Churchill stepped in front of Parliament on 13th May in order to assure himself of the support of the House, the situation was sufficiently strained. This speech changed the situation completely. After a short tense silence, the whole House was deeply moved and burst into applause.

to move here: to propose formally in a debate or parliamentary meeting
House short form of "House of Commons"
inflexible unwilling to change
to prosecute here: to follow or pursue with a view to reaching or accomplishing sth

I beg to move,
That this House welcomes the formation of a Government representing the united and inflexible resolve of the nation to prosecute the war with Germany to a victorious conclusion.
On Friday evening last I received His Majesty's Commission 5 to form a new Administration. It was the evident wish and will of Parliament and the nation that this should be conceived on the broadest possible basis and that it should include all parties, both those who supported the late Government and also the parties of the Opposition. I have completed 10 the most important part of this task. A war cabinet has been formed of five Members, representing, with the Liberal Opposition, the unity of the nation. The three party Leaders have agreed to serve, either in the War Cabinet or in high executive office. The three Fighting Services have been filled. 15 It was necessary that this should be done in one single day, on account of the extreme urgency and rigour of events. A number of other key positions were filled yesterday and I am submitting a further list to His Majesty tonight. I hope to complete the appointment of the principal Ministers during 20 tomorrow. The appointment of the other ministers usually takes a little longer, but I trust that, when Parliament meets again, this part of my task will be completed, and that the Administration will be complete in all respects.

His Majesty's Commission refers to the official transfer of power and authority to Churchill that was granted by King George VI (1895–1952). Immediately after, Churchill set up a **war cabinet** – an all-party coalition consisting of the **three party leaders** (Chamberlain, Attlee and the Liberal Archibald Sinclair) as well as about a dozen **principal Ministers**.

to conceive to devise
Member Member of Parliament
rigour here: extreme seriousness

in all respects to all intents and purposes

Sir, I considered it in the public interest to suggest that the House should be summoned to meet today. Mr. Speaker agreed, and took the necessary steps, in accordance with the powers conferred upon him by the Resolution of the House.
5 At the end of the proceedings today, the Adjournment of the House will be proposed until Tuesday, 21st May, with, of course, provision for earlier meeting, if need be. The business to be considered during that week will be notified to Members at the earliest opportunity. I now invite the House, by
10 the resolution which stands in my name, to record its approval of the steps taken and to declare its confidence in the new Government.

Sir, to form an Administration of this scale and complexity is a serious undertaking in itself, but it must be remembered that
15 we are in the preliminary stage of one of the greatest battles in history, that we are in action at many other points in Norway and in Holland, that we have to be prepared in the Mediterranean, that the air battle is continuous and that many preparations have to be made here at home. In this crisis I hope I
20 may be pardoned if I do not address the House at any length today. I hope that any of my friends and colleagues, or former colleagues, who are affected by the political reconstruction, will make all allowances for any lack of ceremony with which it has been necessary to act. I would say to the House, as I said
25 to those who have joined this Government: "I have nothing to offer but blood, toil, tears, and sweat."

We have before us an ordeal of the most grievous kind. We have before us many, many long months of struggle and of suffering. You ask, what is our policy? I will say: It is to wage
30 war, by sea, land and air, with all our might and with all the strength that God can give us; to wage war against a monstrous tyranny, never surpassed in the dark, lamentable catalogue of human crime. That is our policy. You ask, what is our aim? I can answer in one word: Victory, victory at all costs,
35 victory in spite of all terror, victory, however long and hard the road may be: for without victory, there is no survival.

Let that be realised: no survival for the British Empire, no survival for all that the British Empire has stood for, no survival for the urge and impulse of the ages, that mankind will
40 move forward towards its goal. But I take up my task with buoyancy and hope. I feel sure that our cause will not be suffered to fail among men. At this time I feel entitled to claim the aid of all, and I say, "Come then, let us go forward together with our united strength."

---

to be summoned to be called

in accordance with in compliance with

to confer sth upon sb to officially assign sth to sb

proceedings here: parliamentary session

adjournment the act of postponing to another time or moving to another place

to notify sth to sb to officially let sb know sth

by the resolution which stands in my name by the formal proposal for action which has been put forward by me

to record one's approval to officially document one's agreement

complexity intricacy

preliminary coming before a more important action or event

to be in action here: to be involved in military combat

reconstruction the activity of building sth again

ordeal a very unpleasant and painful or difficult experience

grievous causing fear or anxiety by threatening great harm

to wage war to fight a war with

monstrous shockingly brutal or cruel

to surpass to exceed

lamentable very bad or distressing

let that be realised let's get that straight

buoyancy an ability to stay happy despite having difficulties

to suffer sth to fail to allow sth to fail

John F. Kennedy: **The Berlin speech (1963)**

Of Irish descent, John Fitzgerald Kennedy was born in Brookline, Massachusetts on May 29, 1917, and was to become the first Roman Catholic President. After the Second World War, The Allied Powers divided Germany into four sectors: American, Russian, British and French. This division was also made in the city of Berlin. The Russian sector which was later to be established as the German Democratic Republic and East Berlin set up a communist regime in contrast to the democracy in the Federal Republic of Germany. On 13 August 1961, the Berlin Wall dividing the city into democratic and communist sectors was erected. When Kennedy visited Berlin in June 1963, the Mayor at that time was Willy Brandt, who would later become the Chancellor of West Germany. Kennedy made a ground-breaking speech offering American solidarity to the citizens of West Germany. A crowd of 120,000 Berliners gathered in front of the Schöneberg Rathaus (City Hall) to hear him speak.

Willy Brandt (1913–1992) belonged to the Social Democratic Party (SPD) and was **Mayor of Berlin** from 1957–1966. From 1969 to 1974, he was the Chancellor of Germany.
Konrad Adenauer (1876–1967) was the **German chancellor** from 1949 until 1963.
At the height of WWII activities in 1942, **General Lucius Clay** was the youngest Army Brigadier General. When sporadic Soviet harassment of wartorn Berlin began in early 1948, Clay acted on his own initiative as CINCEUR (Commander in Chief, European Command) when he ordered 'the airlift begun!'.

distinguished respected or admired
boast proud statement

"civis Romanus sum" Latin: "I am a Roman citizen." With this sentence at the time of the Roman Empire, Roman citizens persecuted abroad used to appeal to their Roman citizenship, which granted them privileges.

I am proud to come to this city as the guest of your distinguished Mayor, who has symbolised throughout the world the fighting spirit of West Berlin. And I am proud to visit the Federal Republic with your distinguished chancellor who for so many years has committed Germany to democracy and freedom and progress, and to come here in the company of my fellow American, General Clay, who has been in this city during its great moments of crisis and will come again if ever needed. Two thousand years ago the proudest boast was "civis Romanus sum". Today, in the world of freedom, the proudest boast is "Ich bin ein Berliner".
I appreciate my interpreter translating my German!

'Vitality and force'

There are many people in the world who really don't understand, or say they don't, what is the great issue between the free world and the Communist world. Let them come to Berlin.
There are some who say that Communism is the wave of the future. Let them come to Berlin.
And there are some who say in Europe and elsewhere we can work with the Communists. Let them come to Berlin.
And there are even a few who say that it is true that Communism is an evil system, but it permits us to make economic

progress. Lass' sie nach Berlin kommen. Let them come to Berlin.

Freedom has many difficulties and democracy is not perfect, but we have never had to put a wall up to keep our people in,
5 to prevent them from leaving us.

I want to say, on behalf of my countrymen, who live many miles away on the other side of the Atlantic, who are far distant from you, that they take the greatest pride that they have been able to share with you, even from a distance, the
10 story of the last 18 years.

I know of no town, no city, that has been besieged for 18 years that still lives with the vitality and the force, and the hope and the determination of the city of West Berlin.

'Part of the main'

15 While the wall is the most obvious and vivid demonstration of the failures of the Communist system, for all the world to see, we take no satisfaction in it, for it is, as your mayor has said, an offence not only against history but an offence against humanity, separating families, dividing husbands
20 and wives and brothers and sisters, and dividing a people who wish to be joined together.

What is true of this city is true of Germany – real, lasting peace in Europe can never be assured as long as one German out of four is denied the elementary right of free men, and
25 that is to make a free choice.

In 18 years of peace and good faith, this generation of Germans has earned the right to be free, including the right to unite their families and their nation in lasting peace, with good will to all people.
30 You live in a defended island of freedom, but your life is part of the main.

So let me ask you as I close, to lift your eyes beyond the dangers of today, to the hopes of tomorrow, beyond the freedom merely of this city of Berlin, or your country of Germany, to
35 the advance of freedom everywhere, beyond the wall to the day of peace with justice, beyond yourselves and ourselves to all mankind.

'Front lines'

40 Freedom is indivisible, and when one man is enslaved, all are not free.

The story of the last 18 years At the end of World War II, Germany and Berlin were subsequently divided into four sectors: American, British, French and Russian.

to besiege to surround a place, esp. with an army, to prevent people or supplies getting in or out

offence an illegal act

to assure to cause something to be certain

part of the main quoted from John Donne: "No man is an island, entire of itself; every man is a piece of the continent, a part of the main ..."

indivisible not able to be separated from sth else or into smaller parts

When all are free, then we can look forward to that day when this city will be joined as one and this country and this great continent of Europe in a peaceful and hopeful globe.

When that day finally comes, as it will, the people of West Berlin can take sober satisfaction in the fact that they were in ₅ the front lines for almost two decades. All free men, wherever they may live, are citizens of Berlin, and, therefore, as a free man, I take pride in the words "Ich bin ein Berliner".

sober solemn, serious

Biographies

Marc Antony (83 BC–30 BC) was a Roman politician and general. He was an important supporter of Gaius Julius Caesar as a military commander and administrator. After Caesar's assassination, Antony allied with Octavian and Marcus Aemilius Lepidus to form an official triumvirate, which modern scholars have labelled the second triumvirate. The triumvirate broke up in 33 BC. Disagreement between Octavian and Antony turned to civil war in 31 BC. Antony was defeated by Octavian at the naval Battle of Actium and then in a short land battle at Alexandria. He committed suicide, and his lover, Queen Cleopatra VII of Egypt, killed herself soon afterwards.

Abraham Lincoln (1809–1865) was the 16th President from 1861 to 1865. The son of a Kentucky frontierman, he had to struggle to make a living and to have the chance to learn. In 1858, Lincoln ran against Stephen A. Douglas for Senator. Although he lost the election, his debates with Douglas gained him a national reputation that won him the Republican nomination for President in 1860. As an outspoken opponent of the expansion of slavery and a political leader in the western states, he was elected President later that year. As President, he built the Republican Party into a strong national organisation. Furthermore, he rallied most of the northern Democrats to the Union cause. On January 1, 1863, he issued the Emancipation Proclamation that declared forever free those slaves within the Confederacy. The Civil War was fought under his Presidency and he was assassinated at Ford's Theatre in Washington by an actor shortly after the war had ended.

Winston Churchill (1874–1965) was one of the most important leaders in modern British and world history. He was elected as a Member of Parliament in 1900 for the Conservative Party; however, in 1904, he became a member of the Liberal Party. In 1925, he changed parties again and rejoined the Conservatives. When he helped break the Great Strike in 1926, he became the enemy of many trade union members and workers. In 1940, he was elected Prime Minister and led Britain through World War II. In 1945, he lost the election because it seemed that many Britons did not believe he would be able to lead them in the after-war times. However, in 1951, he was re-elected as Prime Minister, serving until 1955. He was not only an outstanding politician but also a brilliant historian and writer. During his second term in office, he even won the Nobel Prize in Literature (1953) for his many books on history.

John Fitzgerald Kennedy (1917–1963) was of Irish descent. Graduating from Harvard in 1940, he entered the Navy. In 1943, when his PT boat was rammed and sunk by a Japanese destroyer, Kennedy, despite grave injuries, led the survivors through perilous waters to safety. Back from the war, he became a Democratic Congressman from the Boston area, advancing in 1953 to the Senate. In 1961, Kennedy became the first Roman Catholic President (35th President). As President, he set out to redeem his campaign pledge to get America moving again. His economic programs launched the country on its longest sustained expansion since World War II; before his death, he laid plans for a massive assault on persisting pockets of privation and poverty. Responding to ever more urgent demands, he took vigorous action in the cause of equal rights, calling for new civil rights legislation. He was shot in Dallas, Texas.

The Hispanic American dream

Hillary R. Clinton: America's best days are still ahead (2005)

Senator Hillary Clinton made the following speech at the annual conference of the NCLR (National Council of La Raza), the largest Hispanic civil rights organization on July 18, 2005 in Philadelphia.

[…] And what an appropriate place. Because for many of us as we look back on American history, Philadelphia is the birthplace of the American dream.

You know, just think, a few blocks away from here, some very
5 visionary men were drafting the Declaration of Independence, creating an entirely new kind of government, trying to determine what this new government would be founded on. And really what they decided, I think it would be fair to say, came to be called the American Dream.

10 Because they believed, as we believe, that we are, each of us, men and women alike, endowed by God with the rights to life, liberty and the pursuit of happiness. There had never been a government before that had ever said, every individual has the spark of their creator and every individual has the
15 right to life, liberty and the pursuit of happiness.

Now, it has taken us a long time to make the progress we should to fulfill that dream for many, many of our people. But without the dream, we could have never made the progress. And since our country's founding, Hispanic Americans from
20 missionaries and admirals to Nobel laureates and astronauts have not only been seeking the American Dream for themselves, but helping to preserve and expand it for others.

And over the past 229 years since that dream was given language and life here in Philadelphia, we have learned that our
25 country is at its best when we work together to make sure that the American Dream is accessible to all who are willing

NCLR The National Council of La Raza, the largest Hispanic civil rights organisation, was established to reduce poverty and discrimination and to improve opportunities for Hispanic Americans.

La Raza literally "the race", here: a Hispanic advocacy organisation that is primarily concerned with securing increased access to mainstream American society for illegal aliens

to draft to write a preliminary that will need to be changed before it is in its finished form
to endow sb with sth to give inborn qualities or talents to sb
pursuit a goal that sb tries to achieve in a determined way
spark a trace of life that activates greater potential

laureate sb who has been given an important prize or honour, esp. the Nobel Prize

to work hard and be responsible for themselves and their families. That's why La Raza has always been so important. Because for 40 years, you have been working to break down the barriers that too often wall people off from the American Dream. And I am grateful for that work. It is not finished, 5 however. [...]

And as I think about what our agenda in Washington should be, I think number one we have to provide our young people with high-quality education, training and English instruction to prepare them for adulthood. We have to protect every 10 child's health and we have to take action against silent epidemics like lead poisoning and asthma that can steal their future even before it begins. We have to offer healthcare to families and children, because sick kids can't go to school and sick adults can't go to work. And we have to ensure that 15 everyone has a fair shake in this economy. Now, these are not just my priorities. They're not even just your priorities. They're not even just Hispanic or Latino priorities. These are American priorities. And it is incredibly important that we recommit ourselves to these priorities. 20

Let's start with education, because it has already been mentioned today. We have known from the beginning of this country that education was the key to advancement, to mobility, to success in our society, that if we were trying to have a country based on merit, instead of where you were born, 25 what family you were born into, whether you had land, whether you had money, if it was going to be based on merit, there was only one key to that merit and that had to be education.

But whether our children, and when I say children I mean all 30 of our children, will be able to meet the challenges of the future is an open question because we are no longer competing Pennsylvania vs. New York, California vs. Florida, we are competing the United States vs. China, the United States vs. India, vs. Russia, Europe, vs. Latin America. We are in a global 35 competition for the future. And the quality of education will determine, not just whether an individual can win and compete, but whether all of us, as Americans, can win and compete. I worry about this because to me, whether or not we get the educational challenge right is as important as anything 40 else we're doing in America right now.

Now it is not just about schools. Schools are very important, but it is also about family and community. It is about the lessons that people pass on to their own children about how important education is, how important learning is for the 45

agenda a list of problems or subjects that a government, organisation, etc. is planning to deal with

advancement progress or development in your job, level of knowledge, etc.

to meet a challenge to successfully deal with sth that tests strength, skill, or ability, esp. in a way that is interesting or difficult

future. And we need to make it easier, not harder, for American families of every background, to make sure their children graduate from high school and go on and succeed in college. [...]

5 Now, I understand yesterday that you held a rally and you featured four high-school students from Arizona and these four students designed a remote-controlled vehicle and they beat the entries from the MIT students in a national competition. Now, I want to be sure to get their names because I am
10 going to find somebody to make sure that these four people go to college while we're waiting to get the doors open for everybody else.

All we hear these days is how China and India are graduating more engineers, how they're doing better in math and science.
15 It makes absolutely no sense to take these four bright young people and slam shut the doors to college. That is why I am a proud co-sponsor of the DREAM Act. We want to make it possible for the 65,000 undocumented young people who graduate from our high schools each year to receive in-state tuition
20 rates, and to pursue their own dreams. And I hope with your help, we will make that DREAM Act a reality this year.

But for every poor student that we can point to with pride, there are hundreds of children whose potential is being squandered because they have health problems that we are
25 not tending to. And I know, particularly, that lead contamination harms the development and intelligence of almost a million American children. And Hispanic children are twice as likely to be affected.

Now, lead poisoning is completely preventable, if landlords
30 and parents know the risks and take the action necessary to remove the threat. If we do not take that action, lead poisoning undermines the intellectual ability and the learning capacity of otherwise perfectly bright, normal children. That's why I mention it to you, because I will soon be introducing
35 legislation to give incentives to homeowners and landlords to engage in the safe removal of lead-based hazards. I want your help on this because no child's dream should be ended when he is a toddler because of lead paint poisoning in a situation over which he and his family have very little con-
40 trol, if any.

I also want your help to take on asthma. We are in the middle of an asthma epidemic.

Asthma rates doubled between 1985 and 2005 and no community is being hit harder than the Latino community. In
45 my own state, in New York City, one in every three asthma

rally a large public meeting, esp one that is held outdoors to support a political cause

MIT Massachusetts Institute of Technology

DREAM Act "Development, Relief, and Education for Alien Minors", introduced in November 2005, is a piece of federal legislation that (if passed) would facilitate access to college for hard-working and talented un-documented immigrant students in the U.S.

to squander to carelessly waste, esp. money, time opportunities

incentive sth positive that encourages you to do sth
hazard sth that may be dangerous, or cause health problems

sufferers is Hispanic, and in some communities, like East Harlem, New York, one out of every three Puerto Rican children is asthmatic. And, because of the problems in our health care system, many of these children are not getting adequate treatment. 5

So I am going to be introducing legislation to provide money that will go to researchers to help patients better manage their asthma and we must do a better job of understanding what causes this disease, what contributes to this disease, and I want the money to go to medically underserved communi- 10 ties and require researchers to researchers to collaborate with nonprofit organizations like La Raza and schools so we can help these children stay in school and learn and help them have a brighter future.

But of course, this is part of a larger problem about our health 15 care system. You remember, I tried to do a few things about health care some years ago, and we were not successful. But the problem has not gone away. We still have a growing number of uninsured people and even for people like many of us who have insurance, the cost of the insurance keeps go- 20 ing up. Nearly 24 percent of Hispanic children, let's say a quarter, of Hispanic children, and almost one third of Hispanics under 65, are uninsured.

staggering causing great dismay, shock or surprise

Now these are staggering statistics. And the results are that oftentimes people don't get the treatment they should until 25 the very end of, you know just waiting and trying to save the money, and then they end up in an emergency room. It makes no sense. It costs money, people don't get taken care of the way that they should, even sometimes families have to go into bankruptcy trying to pay the medical bills. There's a tre- 30 mendous amount of waste, a waste of money, a waste of the future that people should have. And I am going to be working hard to make sure we do something about health care.

[...] Now finally, I hope that we can begin creating good paying jobs again in America. We have not created one net new 35 job in America in the past four years. Now I would very much

my husband i.e. Bill Jefferson Clinton, 42nd President of the United States (1993–2001)
surplus more than what is needed or used
broadband a system of connecting computers to the Internet and moving information at a very high speed

like to go back to the economic policies of my husband where we had a balanced budget, where we had a surplus, where we had people going to work. And we can also be investing in new research for new kinds of jobs that can come from broad- 40 band and wireless services and energy technology. There are so many opportunities out there.

And there isn't any group in America that works harder than immigrants. And I know how much money immigrants send home from America to their home countries to help their 45 families and I am a proud co-sponsor on two pieces of legislation that we need your support and voices on.

The first is the International Remittances Services Enhancement and Protection Act. That would remove the regulatory
5 barriers that make it harder for poor people to access low cost credit services. And the second is the Money Wire Act. That will foster transparency in the money transfer industry; it will lower the cost of sending money home and it will give immigrants the information they need to have.

10 You know, on average, I don't need to tell you this but on average, immigrants send home two hundred dollars a month, despite earnings that add up to less than $25,000 a year. Now, in my mind that is the very definition of family values and I'm going to do all I can to pass this legislation,
15 both of those Acts, so that we can reward people who are working hard and playing by the rules.

[…] I hope that […] young people […] will put in the effort to do the best they can in school. That they will put in the effort to make a positive contribution to their community, that
20 they will understand what those of us who have come before have maybe taken for granted, that we can be individually successful but as Americans, as inheritors of this proud dream that was birthed here in this city so long ago, we should never settle just for personal success. We should understand we
25 are all enhanced when everyone does better, when everyone is given the opportunity to live up to his or her God-given potential.

You have made America stronger for all of us, and together I believe we can build an America that is stronger for those
30 who come after us. That is worthy of our highest ideals and keeps faith with the next generation of Americans who come here, who are here, who believe with all their hearts that America's best days are still ahead.

Thank you all so very much, God bless you!

to foster to help sth develop over a period of time through continual encouragement

inheritor sb who takes over sth from an ancestor

to enhance to improve, make better

George W. Bush Jr.: The United States must secure its borders (2006)

On May 13, 2006 President George W. Bush Jr. explained his ideas for solving the problem of illegal immigration to the American people in the following televised speech.

Good evening. I've asked for a few minutes of your time to discuss a matter of national importance – the reform of America's immigration system.

The issue of immigration stirs intense emotions, and in recent weeks, Americans have seen those emotions on display. On the streets of major cities, crowds have rallied in support of those in our country illegally. At our southern border, others have organized to stop illegal immigrants from coming in. Across the country, Americans are trying to reconcile these contrasting images. And in Washington, the debate over immigration reform has reached a time of decision. Tonight, I will make it clear where I stand, and where I want to lead our country on this vital issue.

We must begin by recognizing the problems with our immigration system. For decades, the United States has not been in complete control of its borders. As a result, many who want to work in our economy have been able to sneak across our border, and millions have stayed.

Once here, illegal immigrants live in the shadows of our society. Many use forged documents to get jobs, and that makes it difficult for employers to verify that the workers they hire are legal. Illegal immigration puts pressure on public schools and hospitals, it strains state and local budgets, and brings crime to our communities. These are real problems. Yet we must remember that the vast majority of illegal immigrants are decent people who work hard, support their families, practice their faith, and lead responsible lives. They are a part of American life, but they are beyond the reach and protection of American law.

We're a nation of laws, and we must enforce our laws. We're also a nation of immigrants, and we must uphold that tradition, which has strengthened our country in so many ways. These are not contradictory goals. America can be a lawful society and a welcoming society at the same time. We will fix the problems created by illegal immigration, and we will deliver a system that is secure, orderly, and fair. So I support comprehensive immigration reform that will accomplish five clear objectives.

to rally to meet or bring people together to support sth, esp. an idea or a political party

to reconcile sb to sth to make sb able to accept a difficult or unpleasant situation

to sneak to move secretly or quietly in order to avoid being seen or heard

to forge to illegally copy sth, esp. sth printed or written, to make people think it is real

to strain here: to cause difficulty by creating too much work or too many problems which cannot be dealt with easily

to enforce to make people obey a rule or law

First, the United States must secure its borders. This is a basic
responsibility of a sovereign nation. It is also an urgent re-
quirement of our national security. Our objective is straight-
forward: The border should be open to trade and lawful im-
5 migration, and shut to illegal immigrants, as well as criminals,
drug dealers, and terrorists.

I was a governor of a state that has a 1,200-mile border with
Mexico. So I know how difficult it is to enforce the border,
and how important it is. Since I became President, we've in-
10 creased funding for border security by 66 percent, and expanded the Border Patrol from about 9,000 to 12,000 agents.
The men and women of our Border Patrol are doing a fine job
in difficult circumstances, and over the past five years, they
have apprehended and sent home about six million people
15 entering America illegally.

Despite this progress, we do not yet have full control of the
border, and I am determined to change that. Tonight I'm calling on Congress to provide funding for dramatic improve-
ments in manpower and technology at the border. By the
20 end of 2008, we'll increase the number of Border Patrol officers by an additional 6,000. When these new agents are deployed, we'll have more than doubled the size of the Border
Patrol during my presidency.

At the same time, we're launching the most technologically
25 advanced border security initiative in American history. We
will construct high-tech fences in urban corridors, and build
new patrol roads and barriers in rural areas. We'll employ
motion sensors, infrared cameras, and unmanned aerial ve-
hicles to prevent illegal crossings. America has the best tech-
30 nology in the world, and we will ensure that the Border Patrol has the technology they need to do their job and secure
our border.

Training thousands of new Border Patrol agents and bringing
the most advanced technology to the border will take time.
35 Yet the need to secure our border is urgent. So I'm announcing several immediate steps to strengthen border enforcement during this period of transition:

One way to help during this transition is to use the National
Guard. So, in coordination with governors, up to 6,000 Guard
40 members will be deployed to our southern border. The Border Patrol will remain in the lead. The Guard will assist the
Border Patrol by operating surveillance systems, analyzing
intelligence, installing fences and vehicle barriers, building
patrol roads, and providing training. Guard units will not be
45 involved in direct law enforcement activities – that duty will

George W. Bush Jr. was the
governor of Texas from
1995 to 2000. He became
President on January 20,
2001.

to apprehend to catch, to
arrest

to deploy *aufstellen, einsetzen*

to launch to start sth, usually
sth important

National Guard a volunteer
reserve group of the US army
and Air Force. It can be
called into regular service by
the president or the
Congress and is usually
summoned by a state
governor in the case of a
natural desaster or riot.

surveillance the careful
watching of a person or place
suspected of being involved
with criminal activities
intelligence information about
the secret activities of foreign
governments, military plans,
terrorists, etc.

be done by the Border Patrol. This initial commitment of
Guard members would last for a period of one year. After
that, the number of Guard forces will be reduced as new Border Patrol agents and new technologies come online. It is
important for Americans to know that we have enough Guard 5
forces to win the war on terror, to respond to natural disasters,
and to help secure our border.

The United States is not going to militarize the southern border. Mexico is our neighbor, and our friend. We will continue
to work cooperatively to improve security on both sides of 10
the border, to confront common problems like drug traffick-
ing and crime, and to reduce illegal immigration.

Another way to help during this period of transition is
through state and local law enforcement in our border communities. So we'll increase federal funding for state and local 15
authorities assisting the Border Patrol on targeted enforcement missions. We will give state and local authorities the
specialized training they need to help federal officers apprehend and detain illegal immigrants. State and local law enforcement officials are an important part of our border secu- 20
rity and they need to be a part of our strategy to secure our
borders.

The steps I've outlined will improve our ability to catch
people entering our country illegally. At the same time, we
must ensure that every illegal immigrant we catch crossing 25
our southern border is returned home. [...]

Second, to secure our border, we must create a temporary
worker program. The reality is that there are many people on
the other side of our border who will do anything to come to
America to work and build a better life. They walk across 30
miles of desert in the summer heat, or hide in the back of 18-
wheelers to reach our country. This creates enormous pressure on our border that walls and patrols alone will not stop.
To secure the border effectively, we must reduce the numbers
of people trying to sneak across.   35

Therefore, I support a temporary worker program that would
create a legal path for foreign workers to enter our country in
an orderly way, for a limited period of time. This program
would match willing foreign workers with willing American
employers for jobs Americans are not doing. Every worker 40
who applies for the program would be required to pass criminal background checks. And temporary workers must return
to their home country at the conclusion of their stay.

A temporary worker program would meet the needs of our
economy, and it would give honest immigrants a way to pro- 45

vide for their families while respecting the law. A temporary worker program would reduce the appeal of human smugglers, and make it less likely that people would risk their lives to cross the border. It would ease the financial burden on
5 state and local governments, by replacing illegal workers with lawful taxpayers. And above all, a temporary worker program would add to our security by making certain we know who is in our country and why they are here.

Third, we need to hold employers to account for the workers
10 they hire. It is against the law to hire someone who is in this country illegally. Yet businesses often cannot verify the legal status of their employees because of the widespread problem of document fraud. Therefore, comprehensive immigration reform must include a better system for verifying documents
15 and work eligibility. A key part of that system should be a new identification card for every legal foreign worker. This card should use biometric technology, such as digital fingerprints, to make it tamper-proof. A tamper-proof card would help us enforce the law, and leave employers with no excuse
20 for violating it. And by making it harder for illegal immigrants to find work in our country, we would discourage people from crossing the border illegally in the first place.

Fourth, we must face the reality that millions of illegal immigrants are here already. They should not be given an auto-
25 matic path to citizenship. This is amnesty, and I oppose it. Amnesty would be unfair to those who are here lawfully, and it would invite further waves of illegal immigration. [...]

I believe that illegal immigrants who have roots in our country and want to stay should have to pay a meaningful penalty
30 for breaking the law, to pay their taxes, to learn English, and to work in a job for a number of years. People who meet these conditions should be able to apply for citizenship, but approval would not be automatic, and they will have to wait in line behind those who played by the rules and followed the
35 law. What I've just described is not amnesty, it is a way for those who have broken the law to pay their debt to society, and demonstrate the character that makes a good citizen.

Fifth, we must honor the great American tradition of the melting pot, which has made us one nation out of many peoples.
40 The success of our country depends upon helping newcomers assimilate into our society, and embrace our common identity as Americans. Americans are bound together by our shared ideals, an appreciation of our history, respect for the flag we fly, and an ability to speak and write the English lan-
45 guage. English is also the key to unlocking the opportunity of

burden sth that causes extra problems or pressure

fraud the crime of deceiving people in order to gain sth

tamper-proof here: forgery-proof

to assimilate into to act like the members of a particular group in order to be accepted by that group

America. English allows newcomers to go from picking crops to opening a grocery, from cleaning offices to running offices, from a life of low-paying jobs to a diploma, a career, and a home of their own. When immigrants assimilate and advance in our society, they realize their dreams, they renew 5 our spirit, and they add to the unity of America.

Tonight, I want to speak directly to members of the House and the Senate: An immigration reform bill needs to be comprehensive, because all elements of this problem must be addressed together, or none of them will be solved at all. The 10 House has passed an immigration bill. The Senate should act by the end of this month so we can work out the differences between the two bills, and Congress can pass a comprehensive bill for me to sign into law.

America needs to conduct this debate on immigration in a 15 reasoned and respectful tone. Feelings run deep on this issue, and as we work it out, all of us need to keep some things in mind. We cannot build a unified country by inciting people to anger, or playing on anyone's fears, or exploiting the issue of immigration for political gain. We must always remember 20 that real lives will be affected by our debates and decisions, and that every human being has dignity and value no matter what their citizenship papers say.

I know many of you listening tonight have a parent or a grandparent who came here from another country with 25 dreams of a better life. You know what freedom meant to them, and you know that America is a more hopeful country because of their hard work and sacrifice.[...]

Our new immigrants are just what they've always been – people willing to risk everything for the dream of freedom. 30 And America remains what she has always been: the great hope on the horizon, an open door to the future, a blessed and promised land. We honor the heritage of all who come here, no matter where they come from, because we trust in our country's genius for making us all Americans – one na- 35 tion under God.

Thank you, and good night.

bill here: a written proposal for a new law

to incite to deliberately encourage people to fight, argue or get upset

sacrifice the decision to give up sth valuable, in order to achieve sth that is more important

heritage the traditional beliefs, values, customs, etc. of a family, country, or society

The black American dream

Malcolm X: The ballot or the bullet (1964)

On April 12, 1964, eight months after the March on Washington and Martin Luther King's famous speech "I have a dream", Malcolm X gave the following speech demanding full civil rights for Black Americans.

[...] Whether you are – Whether you are a Christian, or a Muslim, or a Nationalist, we all have the same problem. They don't hang you because you're a Baptist; they hang you 'cause you're black. They don't attack me because I'm a Muslim;
5 they attack me 'cause I'm black. They attack all of us for the same reason; all of us catch hell from the same enemy. We're all in the same bag, in the same boat. We suffer political oppression, economic exploitation, and social degradation – all of them from the same enemy. The government has failed us;
10 you can't deny that. Anytime you live in the twentieth century, 1964, and you walkin' around here singing "We Shall Overcome," the government has failed us.
This is part of what's wrong with you – you do too much singing. Today it's time to stop singing and start swinging.
15 You can't sing up on freedom, but you can swing up on some freedom. Cassius Clay can sing, but singing didn't help him to become the heavyweight champion of the world; swinging helped him become the heavyweight champion. This government has failed us; the government itself has failed us,
20 and the white liberals who have been posing as our friends have failed us.
And once we see that all these other sources to which we've turned have failed, we stop turning to them and turn to ourselves. We need a self help program, a do-it – a-do-it-yourself
25 philosophy, a do-it-right-now philosophy, a it's-already-too-late philosophy. This is what you and I need to get with, and the only time – the only way we're going to solve our problem is with a self-help program. Before we can get a self-help program started we have to have a self-help philosophy.
30 Black Nationalism is a self-help philosophy. What's so good about it? You can stay right in the church where you are and still take Black Nationalism as your philosophy. You can stay in any kind of civic organization that you belong to and still

ballot the piece of paper used to make a secret vote, here: the right to vote

to catch hell (*AmE sl*) to be blamed or punished
degradation lowering in dignity, status or conditions
to fail sb to not do what sb has trusted you to do

"We Shall Overcome" a protest song which was written in 1960 by Pete Seeger to an old traditional tune, which was especially popular during the Civil Rights Movement in the US

Cassius Clay the former name of Muhammad Ali (*1942), a US boxer who became world heavyweight champion in 1964, and then again in 1974 and 1978. He changed his name when he became a Muslim in 1964.

Black Nationalism a political and social movement arising in the 1960's among Afro-Americans in the United States. It emphasized cultural, political, and economic independence for Afro-Americans.

division here: disagreement among the members of a larger group that makes them form smaller opposing groups

pattern here: the usual way of thinking or acting

sit-in a type of protest in which people refuse to leave a place until their demands are agreed to
chump (infml) sb who is naive and easily deceived

hypocritical behaving in a way that is different from what you claim to believe

hypocrite sb who pretends to have certain beliefs or opinions that they do not really have

take black nationalism as your philosophy. You can be an atheist and still take black nationalism as your philosophy. This is a philosophy that eliminates the necessity for division and argument. 'Cause if you're black you should be thinking black, and if you are black and you not thinking black at this 5 late date, well I'm sorry for you.

Once you change your philosophy, you change your thought pattern. Once you change your thought pattern, you change your – your attitude. Once you change your attitude, it changes your behavior pattern and then you go on into some 10 action. As long as you gotta sit-down philosophy, you'll have a sit-down thought pattern, and as long as you think that old sit-down thought you'll be in some kind of sit-down action. They'll have you sitting in everywhere. It's not so good to refer to what you're going to do as a "sit-in." That right there 15 castrates you. Right there it brings you down. What – What goes with it? What – Think of the image of a someone sitting. An old woman can sit. An old man can sit. A chump can sit. A coward can sit. Anything can sit. Well you and I been sitting long enough, and it's time today for us to start doing 20 some standing, and some fighting to back that up.

When we look like – at other parts of this earth upon which we live, we find that black, brown, red, and yellow people in Africa and Asia are getting their independence. They're not getting it by singing "We Shall Overcome." No, they're get- 25 ting it through nationalism. It is nationalism that brought about the independence of the people in Asia. Every nation in Asia gained its independence through the philosophy of nationalism. Every nation on the African continent that has gotten its independence brought it about through the phi- 30 losophy of nationalism. And it will take black nationalism – that to bring about the freedom of 22 million Afro-Americans here in this country where we have suffered colonialism for the past 400 years.

America is just as much a colonial power as England ever was. 35 America is just as much a colonial power as France ever was. In fact, America is more so a colonial power than they because she's a hypocritical colonial power behind it.

What is 20th – What do you call second class citizenship? Why, that's colonization. Second class citizenship is nothing 40 but 20th century slavery. How you gonna tell me you're a second class citizen? They don't have second class citizenship in any other government on this earth. They just have slaves and people who are free. Well this country is a hypocrite. They try and make you think they set you free by calling you 45 a second class citizen. No, you're nothing but a 20th century slave.

Just as it took nationalism to move – to remove colonialism from Asia and Africa, it'll take black nationalism today to re-
5 move colonialism from the backs and the minds of 22 million Afro-Americans here in this country.

And 1964 looks like it might be the year of the ballot or the bullet.

Why does it look like it might be the year of the ballot or the
10 bullet? Because Negroes have listened to the trickery, and the lies, and the false promises of the white man now for too long. And they're fed up. They've become disenchanted. They've become disillusioned. They've become dissatisfied, and all of this has built up frustrations in the black commu-
15 nity that makes the black community throughout America today more explosive than all of the atomic bombs the Russians can ever invent. Whenever you got a racial powder keg sitting in your lap, you're in more trouble than if you had an atomic powder keg sitting in your lap. When a racial powder
20 keg goes off, it doesn't care who it knocks out the way. Understand this, it's dangerous.

And in 1964 this seems to be the year, because what can the white man use now to fool us after he put down that march on Washington? And you see all through that now. He tricked
25 you, had you marching down to Washington. Yes, had you marching back and forth between the feet of a dead man named Lincoln and another dead man named George Washington singing "We Shall Overcome." He made a chump out of you. He made a fool out of you. He made you think
30 you were going somewhere and you end up going nowhere but between Lincoln and Washington.

So today, our people are disillusioned. They've become disenchanted. They've become dissatisfied, and in their frustrations they want action. [...]
35 This is why I say it's the ballot or the bullet. It's liberty or it's death. It's freedom for everybody or freedom for nobody. America today finds herself in a unique situation.

Historically, revolutions are bloody. Oh, yes, they are. They haven't never had a blood-less revolution, or a non-violent
40 revolution. That don't happen even in Hollywood. You don't have a revolution in which you love your enemy, and you don't have a revolution in which you are begging the system of exploitation to integrate you into it. Revolutions overturn systems. Revolutions destroy systems.
45 A revolution is bloody, but America is in a unique position.

disenchanted disappointed in sb or sth, and no longer believing that they are good

powder keg *lit*: a small barrel for holding gunpowder; *fig*: a potentially dangerous situation from which violence or trouble could suddenly erupt

March on Washington reference to the great March on Washington (August 28, 1963), when about 250,000 people (black and white) gathered to demonstrate for a more effective Civil Rights legislation and equal opportunities for Blacks. Its most famous leader was Martin Luther King.

Abraham Lincoln (1809–1865), President of the US from 1861 to 1865, announced the Emancipation Proclamation, by which all slaves in the US became free citizens in 1863.

George Washington (1732–1799) was the first President of the US, from 1789 to 1797.

Russian Revolution
the events of 1917, when the Russian people overthrew their tsar before the communists took over under the leadership of Lenin

Chinese Revolution
(1911–1912) revolution which led to the founding of the Republic of China

French Revolution the revolution which began in France in 1789. The French king and queen, and many other people of high rank were killed and France became a republic.

Cuban Revolution (1953–1959) the overthrow of Batista's regime and the establishment of a new Cuban government led by Fidel Castro

American Revolution also the American War of Independence (1775–1783), the war in which people in Britain's colonies in North America became independent and established the United States of America

to divide and conquer to defeat or control people by making them argue with each other instead of opposing you

She's the only country in history in a position actually to become involved in a blood-less revolution. The – The Russian revolution was bloody; Chinese revolution was bloody; French revolution was bloody; Cuban revolution was bloody; and there was nothing more bloody then the American Revolution. But today this country can become involved in a revolution that won't take bloodshed. All she's got to do is give the black man in this country everything that's due him – everything. 5

I hope that the white man can see this, 'cause if he don't see 10 it you're finished. If you don't see it you're going to be coming – you're going to become involved in some action in which you don't have a chance. And we don't care anything about your atomic bomb; it's – it's useless because other countries have atomic bombs. When two or three different coun- 15 tries have atomic bombs, nobody can use them, so it means that the white man today is without a weapon. If you're gonna – If you want some action, you gotta come on down to Earth. And there's more black people on Earth than there are white people on Earth. [...] 20

So, I say in my conclusion the only way we're going to solve it – we gotta unite in unity and harmony, and Black Nationalism is the key. How we gonna overcome the tendency to be at each other's throats that always exists in our neighborhoods? And the reason this tendency exists, the strategy of 25 the white man has always been divide and conquer. He keeps us divided in order to conquer us. He tells you I'm for separation and you're for integration to keep us fighting with each other. No, I'm not for separation and you're not for integration. What you and I is for is freedom. Only you think that 30 integration will get you freedom, I think separation will get me freedom. We both got the same objective. We just got different ways of getting at it. [...]

It'll be – It'll be the – the ballot or it'll be the bullet. It'll be liberty or it'll be death. And if you're not ready to pay that 35 price don't use the word freedom in your vocabulary. [...]

Ossie Davis: Our shining black prince (1965)

After the assassination of Malcolm X, a black leader in the US who had worked to improve the social and economic position of black people (cf. p. 41), the following eulogy was delivered by Ossie Davis at his funeral at the Faith Temple Church of God in Harlem, New York on February 27, 1965.

Harlem an area of New York City in northeast Manhattan where many Afro-American and Hispanic people live

Here – at this final hour, in this quiet place – Harlem has come to bid farewell to one of its brightest hopes – extinguished now, and gone from us forever. For Harlem is where he worked and where he struggled and fought – his home of
5 homes, where his heart was, and where his people are – and it is, therefore, most fitting that we meet once again – in Harlem – to share these last moments with him.

to extinguish to put out a fire or light; here: to end the existence of

For Harlem has ever been gracious to those who have loved her, have fought for her and have defended her honor even
10 to the death. It is not in the memory of man that this beleaguered, unfortunate, but nonetheless proud community has found a braver, more gallant young champion than this Afro-American who lies before us – unconquered still.

beleaguered experiencing a lot of problems or criticism

gallant courageous

I say the word again, as he would want me to: Afro-American
15 – Afro-American Malcolm, who was a master, was most meticulous in his use of words. Nobody knew better than he the power words have over minds of men.

meticulous precise, very careful

Malcolm had stopped being a Negro years ago. It had become too small, too puny, too weak a word for him. Malcolm was
20 bigger than that. Malcolm had become an Afro-American, and he wanted – so desperately – that we, that all his people, would become Afro-Americans, too.

puny small and weak

There are those who will consider it their duty, as friends of the Negro people, to tell us to revile him, to flee, even from
25 the presence of his memory, to save ourselves by writing him out of the history of our turbulent times.

to revile to express hatred of sb or sth

Many will ask what Harlem finds to honor in this stormy, controversial and bold young captain – and we will smile. Many will say turn away – away from this man; for he is not
30 a man but a demon, a monster, a subverter and an enemy of the black man – and we will smile. They will say that he is of hate – a fanatic, a racist – who can only bring evil to the cause for which you struggle! And we will answer and say to them: Did you ever talk to Brother Malcolm? Did you ever touch
35 him or have him smile at you? Did you ever really listen to him? Did he ever do a mean thing? Was he ever himself associated with violence or any public disturbance? For if you

controversial causing a lot of disagreement, because many people have strong opinions about the subject being discussed
subverter sb who tries to destroy the power and influence of a government or the established system

did, you would know him. And if you knew him, you would know why we must honor him: Malcolm was our manhood, our living, black manhood!

This was his meaning to his people. And, in honoring him, we honor the best in ourselves. Last year, from Africa, he 5 wrote these words to a friend: My journey, he says, is almost ended, and I have a much broader **scope** than when I started out, which I believe will add new life and dimension to our struggle for freedom and honor and dignity in the States.

I am writing these things so that you will know for a fact the 10 **tremendous** sympathy and support we have among the African States for our human rights struggle. The main thing is that we keep a united front wherein our most valuable time and energy will not be wasted fighting each other.

However we may have differed with him – or with each other 15 about him and his value as a man – let his going from us serve only to bring us together, now.

Consigning these mortal remains to earth, the common mother of all, secure in the knowledge that what we place in the ground is no more now a man – but a **seed** – which, after 20 the winter of our discontent, will come forth again to meet us.

And we will know him then for what he was and is – a prince – our own black shining prince! – who didn't hesitate to die, because he loved us so. 25

scope here: the range of one's thoughts, ideas or actions

tremendous extraordinarily great in size or amount

seed a small, hard object produced by plants, from which a new plant of the same kind can grow

Robert F. Kennedy: I have some very sad news for all of you (1968)

Martin Luther King (1929–1968) a black US religious leader who became the most important leader of the Civil Rights Movement and who worked hard to achieve social changes for black people

When Robert F. Kennedy was informed about the assassination of Martin Luther King, he delivered the following speech to the American people on April 4, 1968.

Ladies and Gentlemen,
I'm only going to talk to you just for a minute or so this evening, because I have some – some very sad news for all of you – Could you lower those signs, please? – I have some very sad news for all of you, and, I think, sad news for all of our 5 fellow citizens, and people who love peace all over the world; and that is that Martin Luther King was shot and was killed tonight in Memphis, Tennessee.

Martin Luther King dedicated his life to love and to justice
between fellow human beings. He died in the cause of that
effort. In this difficult day, in this difficult time for the United States, it's perhaps well to ask what kind of a nation we are
5 and what direction we want to move in. For those of you
who are black – considering the evidence evidently is that
there were white people who were responsible – you can be
filled with bitterness, and with hatred, and a desire for revenge.

10 We can move in that direction as a country, a greater polarization – black people amongst blacks, and white amongst
whites, filled with hatred toward one another. Or we can
make an effort, as Martin Luther King did, to understand,
and to comprehend, and replace that violence, that stain of
15 bloodshed that has spread across our land, with an effort to
understand, compassion and love.

For those of you who are black and are tempted to fill with –
be filled with hatred and mistrust of the injustice of such an
act, against all white people, I would only say that I can also
20 feel in my own heart the same kind of feeling. I had a member of my family killed, but he was killed by a white man.

But we have to make an effort in the United States. We have
to make an effort to understand, to get beyond, or go beyond
these rather difficult times.

25 My favourite poem, my – my favourite poet was Aeschylus.
And he once wrote:

Even in our sleep, pain which cannot forget
falls drop by drop upon the heart,
until, in our own despair,
30 *against our will,*
comes wisdom
through the awful grace of God.

What we need in the United States is not division; what we
need in the United States is not hatred; what we need in the
35 United States is not violence and lawlessness, but is love, and
wisdom, and compassion toward one another, and a feeling
of justice toward those who still suffer within our country,
whether they be white or whether they be black.

So I ask you tonight to return home, to say a prayer for the
40 family of Martin Luther King – yeah, it's true – but more im-
portantly to say a prayer for our own country, which all of us
love – a prayer for understanding and that compassion of
which I spoke.

polarization division into clearly separate groups with opposite beliefs

stain a mark that is difficult to remove, esp. one made by blood, used here to denote a shameful act
compassion a strong feeling of sympathy for sb who is suffering

"I had a member of my family killed" reference to the assassination of the speaker's brother, John F. Kennedy (1917–1963), a US politician in the Democratic Party, also known as JFK, who was President of the US from 1961 to 1963

Aeschylus (?525–?456 BC) ancient Greek writer who was one of the earliest writers to develop the European style of drama, esp. tragedy

division here: disagreement among the members of a group that makes them form smaller opposing groups

We can do well in this country. We will have difficult times. We've had difficult times in the past, but we – and we will have difficult times in the future. It is not the end of violence; it is not the end of lawlessness; and it's not the end of disorder. 5

But the vast majority of white people and the vast majority of black people in this country want to live together, want to improve the quality of our life, and want justice for all human beings that abide in our land.

to abide here: to live in a place

And let's dedicate ourselves to what the Greeks wrote so 10 many years ago: to tame the savageness of man and make gentle the life of this world. Let us dedicate ourselves to that, and say a prayer for our country and for our people.

Thank you very much.

Bill Cosby: It's what you're not doing (2004)

NAACP the National Association for the Advancement of Colored People – an American organization that works for the rights of African-American people

Brown v. Board of Education (1954) was a landmark decision by the United States Supreme Court which explicitly outlawed racial segregation in public schools.

Bill Cosby gave the following speech at the NAACP's Gala in Washington to commemorate the 50th anniversary of Brown v. Board of Education on May 17, 2004.

Ladies and gentlemen,
I really have to ask you to seriously consider what you've heard, and now this is the end of the evening so to speak. I heard a prize fight manager say to his fellow who was losing badly, "David, listen to me. It's not what's he's doing to you. 5 It's what you're not doing."

to drop out to leave a school or university before you have completed your studies

Ladies and gentlemen, these people set – they opened the doors, they gave us the right, and today, ladies and gentlemen, in our cities and public schools we have 50% drop out. In our own neighborhood, we have men in prison. No longer 10 is a person embarrassed because they're pregnant without a husband. No longer is a boy considered an embarrassment if he tries to run away from being the father of the unmarried child.

to hold one's end (up) (infml) to do one's share
to (play) hooky (infml) to stay away from school without permission

Ladies and gentlemen, the lower economic and lower middle 15 economic people are not holding their end in this deal. In the neighborhood that most of us grew up in, parenting is not going on. In the old days, you couldn't hooky school because every drawn shade was an eye. And before your mother got off the bus and to the house, she knew exactly where you had gone, who had gone into the house, and where you got on whatever you had one and where you got it from. Parents don't know that today.

5 I'm talking about these people who cry when their son is standing there in an orange suit. Where were you when he was two? Where were you when he was twelve? Where were you when he was eighteen, and how come you don't know he had a pistol? And where is his father, and why don't you 10 know where he is? And why doesn't the father show up to talk to this boy?

The church is only open on Sunday. And you can't keep asking Jesus to ask doing things for you. You can't keep asking that God will find a way. God is tired of you. God was there when 15 they won all those cases. 50 in a row. That's where God was because these people were doing something. And God said, "I'm going to find a way." I wasn't there when God said it – I'm making this up. But it sounds like what God would do.

We cannot blame white people. White people – white people 20 don't live over there. They close up the shop early. The Korean ones still don't know us as well – they stay open 24 hours. [...]

50 percent drop out rate, I'm telling you, and people in jail, and women having children by five, six different men. Under 25 what excuse? I want somebody to love me. And as soon as you have it, you forget to parent. Grandmother, mother, and great grandmother in the same room, raising children, and the child knows nothing about love or respect of any one of the three of them. All this child knows is "gimme, gimme, 30 gimme." These people want to buy the friendship of a child, and the child couldn't care less. Those of us sitting out here who have gone on to some college or whatever we've done, we still fear our parents. And these people are not parenting. They're buying things for the kid – $500 sneakers – for what? 35 They won't buy or spend $250 on *Hooked on Phonics*.

A Kenneth Clark, somewhere in his home in upstate New York – just looking ahead. Thank God he doesn't know what's going on. Thank God. But these people – the ones up here in the balcony fought so hard. Looking at the incarcerated, these 40 are not political criminals. These are people going around stealing Coca Cola. People getting shot in the back of the head over a piece of pound cake! Then we all run out and are outraged: "The cops shouldn't have shot him." What the hell was he doing with the pound cake in his hand? I wanted a 45 piece of pound cake just as bad as anybody else. And I looked

orange suit an orange uniform prisoners have to wear in US jails

gimme (*sl*) give me
parenting the skill of properly looking after your children

Hooked on Phonics
a commercial brand of educational materials that help children learn to read

Kenneth Clark
(1914–2005) was the first African-American to receive a Ph. D. in Psychology from Columbia University. Together with his wife Mamie Phipps Clark, a fellow psychologist, he played a key role in overturning segregation in schools.

to incarcerate (*fml*) to put sb in prison
pound cake a heavy cake made from flour, sugar, and butter
outraged very angry and shocked

at it and I had no money. And something called parenting said if you get caught with it you're going to embarrass your mother." Not, "You're going to get your butt kicked." No. "You're going to embarrass your mother." "You're going to embarrass your family. In the old days, a girl getting pregnant 5 had to go down South, and then her mother would go down to get her. But the mother had the baby. I said the mother had the baby. The girl didn't have a baby. The mother had the baby in two weeks. We are not parenting.

Ladies and gentlemen, listen to these people. They are show- 10 ing you what's wrong. People putting their clothes on backwards. Isn't that a sign of something going on wrong? Are you not paying attention? People with their hat on backwards, pants down around the crack. Isn't that a sign of something or are you waiting for Jesus to pull his pants up? Isn't it a sign 15 to something when she's got her dress all the was up to the crack – and got all kinds of needles and things going through her body. What part of Africa did this com from? We are not Africans. Those people are not Africans; they don't know a damned thing about Africa. With names like Shaniqua, Shali- 20 gua, Mohammed and all that crap and all of them are in jail. (When we give these kinds names to our children, we give them the strength and inspiration in the meaning of those names. What's the point of giving them strong names if there is not parenting and values backing it up). 25

Brown versus the Board of Education is no longer the white person's problem. We've got to take the neigborhood back. We've got to go in there. Just forget telling your child to go to the Peace Corps. It's right around the corner. It's standing on the corner. It can't speak English. It doesn't want to speak 30 English. I can't even talk the way those people talk. "Why you ain't where you is go, ra." I don't know who these people are. And I blamed the kid until I heard the mother talk. Then I heard the father talk. This is all in the house. You used to talk a certain way on the corner and you got into the house 35 and switched to English. Everybody knows it's important to speak English except these knuckleheads. You can't land a plane with, "Why you ain't …" You can't be a doctor with that kind of crap coming out of your mouth. There is no Bible that has that kind of language. Where did these people 40 get the idea that they're moving ahead on this. Well, they know they're not; they're just hanging out in the same place, five or six generations sitting in the projects when you're just supposed to stay there long enough to get a job and move out. 45

crack (*infml*) the space between sb's buttocks

crap (*sl*) rubbish, sth says that you think is completely wrong or untrue

Peace Corps a US government organization that aims to help poorer countries, by sending them volunteers, who teach skills in education, health, farming, etc.

knucklehead (*spoken AE*) sb stupid

Projects reference to project homes or public housing built by the government for poor people

Now, look, I'm telling you. It's not what they're doing to us. It's what we're not doing. 50 percent drop out. Look, we're raising our own ingrown immigrants. These people are fighting hard to be ignorant. There's no English being spoken,
5 and they're walking and they're angry. Oh God, they're angry and they have pistols and they shoot and they do stupid things. And after they kill somebody, they don't have a plan. Just murder somebody. Boom. Over what? A pizza? [...]
I'm saying Brown versus the Board of Education. We've got to
10 hit the streets, ladies and gentlemen. I'm winding up, now – no more applause. I'm saying, look at the Black Muslims. There are Black Muslims standing on the street corners and they say so forth and so on, and we're laughing at them because they have bean pies and all that, but you don't read, "Black Muslim
15 gunned down while chastising drug dealer." You don't read that? They don't shot down Black Muslims. You understand me. Muslims tell you to get out of the neighborhood. When you want to clear your neighborhood out, first thing you do is go get the Black Muslims, bean pies and all. And your neigh-
20 borhood is then clear. The police can't do it.
I'm telling you Christians, what's wrong with you? Why can't you hit the streets? Why can't you clean it out ourselves? It's our time now, ladies and gentlemen. It is our time. And I've got good news for you. It's not about money. It's about you
25 doing something ordinarily that we do – get in somebody else's business. It's time for you to not accept the language that these people are speaking, which will take them nowhere. What the hell good is Brown V. Board of Education if nobody wants it?
30 What is with young girls getting after some girl who wants to still remain a virgin? Who are these sick black people and where did they come from and why haven't they been parented to shut up? To go up to girls and try to get a club where "you are nobody ..." This is a sickness, ladies and gen-
35 tlemen, and we are not paying attention to these children. These are children. They don't know anything. They're homeless people. All they know how to do is beg. And you give it to them, trying to win their friendship. And what are they good for? And then they stand there in a orange suit and
40 you drop to your knees: "He didn't do anything. He didn't do anything." Yes, he did do it. And you need to have an orange suit on, too.
So, ladies and gentlemen, I want to thank you for the award – and giving me an opportunity to speak because, I mean,
45 this is the future, and all of these people who lined up and

---

to wind sb up to deliberately say or do sth that will annoy or worry, as a joke

Black Muslim a member of a group of black people who believe in the religion of Islam and want a separate black society

bean pie a sweet custard pie commonly associated with the Nation of Islam movement and its spiritual leader Elijah Muhammad. The pies are commonly sold by followers of the religion to raise money for the cause.

to chastise (*fml*) to criticize sb severely

to get a club to get a chance

done – they've got to be wondering what the hell happened. Brown V. Board of Education – these people who marched and were hit in the face with rocks and punched in the face to get an education and we got these knuckleheads walking around who don't want to learn English. I know that you all know it. I just want to get you as angry that you ought to be. When you walk around the neighborhood and you see this stuff, that stuff's not funny. These people are not funny anymore. And that's not my brother. And that's not my sister. They're faking and they're dragging me way down because the state, the city, and all these people have to pick up the tab on them because they don't want to accept that they have to study to get an education.

We have to begin to build in the neighborhood, have restaurants, have cleaners, have pharmacies, have real estate, have medical buildings instead of trying to rob them all. And so, ladies and gentlemen, please, Dorothy Height, where ever she's sitting, she didn't do all that stuff so that she could hear somebody say "I can't stand algebra, I can't stand …" and "what you is." It's horrible.

Basketball players – multimillionaires can't write a paragraph. Football players, multimillionaires, can't read. Yes. Multimillionaires. Well, Brown v. Board of Education, where are we today? It's there. They paved the way. What did we do with it? The White Man, he's laughing – got to be laughing. 50 percent drop out – rest of them in prison. […]

Let's start parenting.

Thank you, thank you.

to pick up the tab to pay for sth, esp. when it is not your responsibility to pay

real estate the business of selling houses or land

Dorothy Irene Height
(*1912) an African-American administrator, educator and social activist who played a key role in the Civil Rights Movement

Biographies

Hillary Rodham Clinton (*1947) (wife of former President William Jefferson Clinton) is a Senator from New York. She graduated from Yale Law School in 1973, was First Lady of Arkansas from 1979–1981 and 1983–1993, then was First Lady of the United States from 1993–2001. Soon after, she was elected to the United States Senate for a term commencing January 3, 2001, then re-elected in 2006 for the term ending January 3, 2013.

George W. Bush Jr. (*1946) is the 43rd President of the United States and the eldest son of former US President, George H.W. Bush. Having served previously as the 47th Governor of Texas from 1995 to 2000, Bush was first elected president in a close and controversial contest in the 2000 presidential election. In October 2001, after the September 11th attacks, Bush declared a "Global War on Terrorism", authorizing first military attacks on Afghanistan and later the invasion of Iraq. Positioning himself as a war president in the midst of the Iraq war, he was able to gain re-election in 2004. However, since then, his approval ratings have declined considerably, due in large part, to his uncompromising stance on Iraq and refusal to accept the proposals for combating global climate change outlined in the Kyoto Protocol.

Malcolm X (1925–1965) was born as Malcolm Little in Omaha, Nebraska as the son of a Baptist minister. Leaving school after the eighth grade, Malcolm made his way to New York, working for a time as a waiter, but in 1946, was sentenced to a ten-year prison term on burglary charges. While in prison Malcolm became an outspoken defender of Muslim doctrines, accepting the basic argument that evil was an inherent characteristic of the "white man's Christian world." Malcolm was shot and killed at the Audubon Ballroom in Harlem, while preparing to speak.

Ossie Davis (1917–2005) was an actor, filmmaker, activist and theatre director. Modern audiences know Ossie Davis from his many appearances in Spike Lee movies, but Davis has made hundreds of appearances in films, plays and TV shows since 1946, when he made his Broadway debut after serving in the US Army during World War II.

Robert Francis Kennedy (1925–1968) graduated from Harvard University in 1948 and from the University of Virginia Law School in 1951, and was the campaign manager for his brother John F. Kennedy's election to the Presidency in 1960. After this, he was the Attorney General of the United States from January 1961 until his resignation September 3, 1964 to run as a candidate for the United States Senate. Elected as a Democrat from New York to the United States Senate, he served from January 3, 1965 until his assassination in 1968 in Los Angeles.

Bill Cosby (*1937) is a comedian, writer and television producer. In 1965, Cosby became the first African-American actor to star in a weekly television drama series, *I Spy* (1965–1968), winning two Emmys. Later series were *The Bill Cosby Show* (1969–1971), *The New Bill Cosby Show* (1972–1973), and *Fat Albert and the Cosby Kids* (1972–1984). As Cliff Huxtable in *The Cosby Show* (1984–1992), he projected a new image of middle-class African-American families, and the programme was one of the most popular and lucrative in television history.

British political forces

Queen Elizabeth II: Annus horribilis (1992)

When in 1992 Queen Elizabeth II celebrated her fortieth year on the throne, the British monarchy was under unprecedented attack. After the shock of several scandals in her family, the Queen faced a further blow when Windsor Castle caught fire in November. Five days later, the Queen was the Lord Mayor's guest to celebrate her anniversary. Her speech that night is unforgettable because in it she accepted criticism for the first time.

1992 is not a year on which I shall look back with undiluted pleasure. In the words of one of my more sympathetic correspondents, it has turned out to be an 'Annus Horribilis'. I suspect that I am not alone in thinking it so. Indeed, I suspect
5 that there are very few people or institutions unaffected by these last months of worldwide turmoil and uncertainty. This generosity and whole-hearted kindness of the Corporation of the City to Prince Philip and me would be welcome at any time, but at this particular moment, in the aftermath of Fri-
10 day's tragic fire at Windsor, it is especially so.
And, after this last weekend, we appreciate all the more what has been set before us today. Years of experience, however, have made us a bit more canny than the lady, less well versed than us in the splendours of City hospitality, who, when she
15 was offered a balloon glass for her brandy, asked for 'only half a glass, please'.
It is possible to have too much of a good thing. A well-meaning Bishop was obviously doing his best when he told Queen Victoria, "Ma'am, we cannot pray too often, nor too fervently,
20 for the Royal Family". The Queen's reply was: "Too fervently, no; too often, yes". I, like Queen Victoria, have always been a believer in that old maxim "moderation in all things".
I sometimes wonder how future generations will judge the events of this tumultuous year. I dare say that history will

undiluted pure, not mixed with anything else or lessened

Annus Horribilis (*Latin*) horrible year

Prince Philip Queen Elizabeth's husband

canny clever, careful, and not easily deceived

Queen Victoria, born in 1819, reigned over Britain for almost 64 years before her death in 1901.

fervent showing great emotion or enthusiasm
moderation the quality of avoiding extremes

take a slightly more moderate view than that of some contemporary commentators. Distance is well-known to lend enchantment, even to the less attractive views. After all, it has the inestimable advantage of hindsight.

hindsight the ability to understand a situation only after it has happened

But it can also lend an extra dimension to judgement, giving 5 it a leavening of moderation and compassion – even of wisdom – that is sometimes lacking in the reactions of those whose task it is in life to offer instant opinions on all things great and small.

No section of the community has all the virtues, neither does 10 any have all the vices. I am quite sure that most people try to do their jobs as best they can, even if the result is not always entirely successful. He who has never failed to reach perfection has a right to be the harshest critic.

There can be no doubt, of course, that criticism is good for 15 people and institutions that are part of public life. No institution – City, Monarchy, whatever – should expect to be free from the scrutiny of those who give it their loyalty and support, not to mention those who don't.

scrutiny careful and thorough examination of sb or sth

But we are all part of the same fabric of our national society 20 and that scrutiny, by one part of another, can be just as effective if it is made with a touch of gentleness, good humour and understanding.

This sort of questioning can also act, and it should do so, as an effective engine for change. The City is a good example of 25 the way the process of change can be incorporated into the stability and continuity of a great institution. I particularly admire, my Lord Mayor, the way in which the City has adapted so nimbly to what the Prayer Book calls "The changes and chances of this mortal life". 30

nimbly able to move quickly and easily with light, neat movements

Prayer Book The Book of Common Prayer is the foundational prayer book of the Church of England.

You have set an example of how it is possible to remain effective and dynamic without losing those indefinable qualities, style and character. We only have to look around this great hall to see the truth of that.

Forty years is quite a long time. I am glad to have had the 35 chance to witness, and to take part in, many dramatic changes in life in this country. But I am glad to say that the magnificent standard of hospitality given on so many occasions to the Sovereign by the Lord Mayor of London has not changed at all. It is an outward symbol of one other unchang- 40 ing factor which I value above all – the loyalty given to me and to my family by so many people in this country, and the Commonwealth, throughout my reign.

Sovereign a king or queen

You, my Lord Mayor, and all those whose prayers – fervent, I hope, but not too frequent – have sustained me through all 45 these years, are friends indeed. Prince Philip and I give you all, wherever you may be, our most humble thanks.

Michael Portillo: The causes of defeat (1997)

Michael Portillo delivered this speech on October 9, 1997 at the Conservative Party Conference in Blackpool. Portillo was the standard bearer of the Euro-sceptic Tory right wing. William Hague became leader but Portillo was regarded by many Tories as the leader in exile.

[...] Let us begin by recognising the scale of our defeat and of our problem. Perhaps as one who went in an instant from being in the Cabinet to being a member of the general public, I am qualified to offer an opinion. I do not accept the view
5 that the Conservatives lost the election of 1997 because we abandoned one-nation Toryism or split the nation. We did not. I will return to that point in a moment. The causes of our defeat were different. I would like to identify what I believe to have been the four principal factors.
10 First, the party became associated increasingly with the most disagreeable messages and thoughts. Much of that linkage was unjustified, but since it is what people thought – what people still think – it must be appreciated as a deeply-felt distaste, rather than momentary irritation. We cannot dis-
15 miss it as mere false perception. Tories were linked to harshness: thought to be uncaring about unemployment, poverty, poor housing, disability and single parenthood; and considered indifferent to the moral arguments over landmines and arms sales. We were thought to favour greed and the unqual-
20 ified pursuit of the free market, with a "devil take the hindmost" attitude.
Second, we abandoned almost completely the qualities of loyalty and the bonds of party without which party effectively ceases to exist. Some of this was ideological. Passions
25 about the future of our country rightly fired people up, but wrongly led them to attack and despise their colleagues. Part of it was egotistical. There were MPs anxious to oblige whenever the media came looking for dissent, seizing the opportunity to be famous for fifteen minutes. But now we are out of
30 government, their views are sought more rarely, and their once-famous faces are fading in the public memory.

perception the way you think about sth and your idea of what it is like

unqualified without limit or control
devil take the hindmost part of the expression "Every man for himself and let the devil take the hindmost" (i.e. the slowest and last in line)

We must re-discover the old instincts that led Tories to support one another and to rally round. Loyalty was never a secret weapon: it was because it was so visible in public, and reinforced in private, that it was so effective. The impact of disunity upon us is clear to see. The party must in the very 5 near future learn again to display the camaraderie and common purpose that are fundamental to a party's prospects. Our new leader, William Hague, has every right to expect our loyalty publicly and privately. If he does not get it, we stand no chance of being re-elected. He has shown that he will 10 lead. Now the party must show that it can be led.

Third, we were thought to be arrogant and out of touch. Much of it may have been no more than personal mannerisms that grated on the public after years in office. Some of it was insensitivity – using the language of economics and high 15 finance when people's jobs and self-esteem were at stake. And when people looked at the composition of our party, they thought it too elderly, or too vulgar, or too out of touch in vocabulary and perceptions, or in some other way, unfamiliar and unrepresentative. 20

Fourth, there was sleaze. I did not believe all that Conservatives were accused of. Even today, I do not think that wrongdoing was any more prevalent in our party than in others, and I expect the rotten boroughs of the Labour Party to prove as much in coming months. But it was certainly bad enough. 25 Sleaze disgraced us in the eyes of the public. Their perception was of corruption and unfitness for public service. Such distasteful perceptions can endure and do us damage for a long time. We should face these issues head on and deal with them. The last years profoundly disappointed our supporters, 30 and disgusted many others. Those of us who were in the parliamentary party, and those of us who were in the government, bear a particular responsibility. [...]

The last word I used was compassion. It is an essential ingredient in Conservatism. We have never lost it, but the world 35 does not believe that. Our reputation has suffered because Conservatives don't wear their hearts on their sleeves. They don't like humbug or display. Their compassion is largely of a practical sort: what can we actually do about the problems that we see around us? That is why Conservatives are to be 40 found in such large numbers working for voluntary organisations. Conservatives have a scepticism about panaceas and about the possibility of government solving problems with a flourish of a pen. But that common sense approach must not mask the fact that concern for others and magnanimity are 45

William Jefferson Hague (*1961) took over as leader of the Conservative Party after John Major's landslide defeat in 1997 then resigned after his own defeat in 2001. He is currently the Conservative Shadow Foreign Secretary.

to grate to annoy sb
insensitivity a lack of understanding for the feelings and situation of others

sleaze immoral behaviour, esp. involving sex or lies

prevalent common at a particular time, place, or among a particular group
borough a town, or part of a large city that is responsible for managing its own affairs

to wear one's heart on one's sleeve to show one's true feelings openly

panacea sth that people think will make everything better and solve all their problems
magnanimity kindness and generosity, esp. towards sb that you have defeated

important qualities of Conservatism, and the instinct for social cohesion transcends the nation. [...]

Now, a word about tactics. There are two things that the Conservative party needs very badly. One, I mentioned, is loyalty.
5 If we cannot re-invent it we cannot govern. The other is patience. I read somewhere that there was frustration with William Hague for not yet coming up with the next big idea. I
accord that remark the prize for the silliest thing said since
the election. The public is not yet ready for such an innova-
10 tion from us, even if a big idea were a thing to be conjured up
at will. People need a rest from us, and we need time to reflect
and listen and come to understand one another better than
we have of late. We certainly need to do a lot about ourselves.
We need better and different organisation. We need a broad
15 and stable financial base. We need to spread our appeal and
attract different sorts of people: different ages, social types,
ethnic groups and cultures.

As for policies, we should be in no great hurry. Get straight
what are our core beliefs. Sort out the confusions and false
20 signals that arose while we were in government. Take a fresh
look in the new circumstances. But there is no call to rush
headlong into inventing new approaches. Our party will renew itself. The new intake of MPs is of extremely high quality.
Just as happened with Labour, those new people will be the
25 engine of our revival. Ministerial office will be theirs, but they
must bide their time patiently too. On the night of the election I wished our new government well, and I do so again.
Conservatives are patriots and we wish to see our country succeed. You will not see us gloat over national reverses, nor talk
30 down our successes, as Labour did when we were the government. We wish to see Britain behaving honourably, being an
influence for good in Europe and the world. We wish to see
the economy remain strong. We do not look to defeat Labour
on the back of national failure. There will be sufficient grounds
35 without that to argue for their removal. I do not underesti-
mate Mr Blair or his achievements. In the years before the
election he skilfully laid bare the areas of life and policy where
the public felt dissatisfied and angry with the Conservatives.
He did not win merely by default, but because of his talent for
40 capturing the public mood. We will learn from that.

Today the Labour government looks very strong and confident. But problems lie ahead. They don't know where they
are headed, and that is dangerous. Mr Blair's great achievement is directionless leadership: he appears to be in control,
45 but no one knows to where he is leading. I have made many

core beliefs the basic ideals that are the most important to sb

to bide one's time to wait until the right moment to do sth

to gloat to show in an annoying way that you are proud of your own success or happy about sb else's failure

mistakes in my career. I suppose we all have. But few people have been consistently wrong on all the great issues that faced our nation over the last fifteen years, as Mr Blair was. Last week, in a speech which was much acclaimed, Mr Blair failed to define the purpose of his government. I perceive no ⁵ ideological roots. I can detect no sense of direction. Labour has a strong sense that it cannot undo what we did. But they do not understand why it was right to do it. They do not accept the politics of freedom and choice that lay behind our agenda. Labour grasped that it had to adopt our rhetoric. But ¹⁰ they will in the end be judged not on what they say but on what they do.

Labour has been guided by the wish to destroy us; and by the determination to be re-elected. That is not a recipe for governing well. You cannot run an administration forever on the ¹⁵ principle that you are unwilling to do anything that offends. You cannot substitute focus group government for cabinet government. Labour is a coalition brought about to win power. That will to win power is the one idea that the members of the government hold in common. But with the passage of ²⁰ time, that will prove an insubstantial glue. The signs of division may today be no bigger than a small crab in a jar, but they will grow.

This government is too bossy, too contemptuous of parliament, too self-satisfied and too little criticised in the media ²⁵ for its own good or for ours. The wheel of fortune turns and that which once appeared fresh, with the passing of time goes to seed. I have set out the many things that we must do to present ourselves again as attractive and suitable for government. ³⁰

But on top of all that, what the Tories need is patience. Principles we already have. Opportunities there will be. Our time will come again.

to go to seed to become less attractive or more worn out, esp. due to age or lack of proper care

Tony Blair: We are the change-maker (2005)

Tony Blair delivered this speech on September 27, 2005 at the Labour Party conference in Brighton.

The question now: How do we secure the future for our party and for our country? The answer lies in understanding why we can celebrate these victories. New Labour was never just a clever way to win. It was a fundamental re-casting of progres-
5 sive politics so that the values we believed in, became relevant to the time we lived in.
In the late 20th century the world had changed, the aspirations of the people had changed; we had to change. We did. We won. And Britain is stronger, fairer, better than on 1st May
10 1997. So what now? The world is on the move again: the change in the early 21st century even greater than that of the late 20th century. So now in turn, we have to change again. Not step back from New Labour but step up to a new mark a changing world is setting for us. The danger of government is
15 fatigue; the benefit, experience. I tell you my conclusion after eight years of being Prime Minister. The challenge we face is not in our values. It is how we put them into practice in a world fast forwarding to the future at unprecedented speed. Over these eight years we have won the battle of values. The
20 age we live in is democratic not deferential. We believe in solidarity. We believe in social justice; in opportunity not for a privileged few but for all, whatever their start in life. We believe in tolerance and respect, in strong communities standing by and standing up for the weak, the sick, the helpless. We
25 all believe this. It's what makes us Labour, from Dennis Skinner through to Tony Blair, though there I'm sure Dennis would want me to say, the similarity ends. In our values, we are united. And the British people share these values. Values don't change. But times do. And now, as before, our values
30 have to be applied anew in changing times. The challenge is policy and not just item by item, but attitude by attitude, direction by direction, in the bold strokes that define the picture not only the small movements that paint the detail. And here the battle is not yet won to secure the future. It is here
35 that the new realities come upon us, snuffing out the lights of victory celebration and urging us to renew yet again.
It is true: we have laid sound foundations. There is only one Government since the war that has cut unemployment, created 2 million more jobs, had eight years of growth without reces-
40 sion and halved interest rates from the previous Government.

1st May 1997 landslide victory for Labour after 18 years of government by the Conservative Party

deferential behaving politely, showing respect

Dennis Skinner (*1932) British politician, Labour member of Parliament since 1970 with left wing views

to snuff out to put out a light or flame

And cut waiting lists in hospitals, improved cancer and heart care, achieved the best ever school results, halved the number of failing schools, seen a five-fold increase in the best ones; achieved record numbers of police and cut crime. Only one Chancellor to have delivered that economic record. This one. 5 Only one Cabinet to have delivered these changes. This one. Only one Government to do it all. Your third term Labour Government. By the end of 2008 for the first time in decades Britain will be investing twice as much in our school children and three times as much in the NHS than ten years before. Only a Labour 10 Government would have done it. No Government but a Labour one would have introduced the New Deal and given one million young people the chance of a decent job. Only a Labour Government would have stopped the scandal of pensioner poverty or introduced the winter fuel allowance. Only a Labour 15 Government would have made a record increase to Child Benefit, or made Sure Start a vital part of some of the poorest communities in the country. Only a Labour Government would ever have brought in a minimum wage, and increased it, and made it such a part of our national life that no Tory will ever 20 dare or even threaten to get rid of it. [...]

Look at Britain's cities. A decade ago in decline. Today, for all the problems that remain, thriving, waterfronts and canals renewed, business up, employment down and slowly, part by part, the regeneration of the inner city underway. Visit the 25 centre of Birmingham. See Liverpool – European City of Culture for 2008. Or Manchester – site of the Commonwealth Games. Visit the Tyne by the Baltic Centre or Glasgow's magnificent Pacific Quay or Cardiff Bay. And then London, scene of triumph and tragedy in successive days in July. And 30 throughout both, it remained indomitable.

It is a privilege to be Prime Minister of such a country with such a capital city. The city of the Olympic Games for Britain in 2012. [...]

And when terrorism struck, the same pride and confidence 35 asserted itself, to the envy and awe of the watching world. London, that day, did Britain proud. This is a country today that increasingly sets the standard. Not for us the malaise of France or the angst of Germany. It's a national pastime to run ourselves down, so occasionally it's worth saying: Britain is a 40 great country and we are proud of it.

So what is the challenge? It is that change is marching on again. Perhaps our children more readily understand this and embrace it than we do. How quickly has the ipod entered the language and the reality of our lives? With what sense of near 45

Chancellor Lord Chancellor, at the time of the speech: Charles Falconer

NHS (National Health Service) public healthcare system in Britain

New Deal program reforms launched by Tony Blair and Gordon Brown on 14th April, 2005 in order to secure the New Labour legacy

winter fuel allowance annual payment to help people aged 60 and over with heating costs
Child Benefit money paid to parents to help with the cost of raising a child
Sure Start government program designed to ensure the best start in life for every child

Commonwealth Games held in Manchester in 2002
Tyne river in the north of England
Baltic Centre Museum of Contemporary Art
Pacific Quay development on the site of the former Glasgow garden festival
Cardiff Bay longest waterfront development in Europe

On **7th July 2005** four bombings in London killed 52 commuters and four suicide bombers.

indomitable unable to be beaten or put down

wonder was the fax machine greeted, just a few years ago, and already overtaken? A baby is born. The father takes a photo on his mobile. In seconds relatives around the world can see, and celebrate. A different world to the one we were born into.
5 Faster, more exciting, yet with that come threats too. The pace of change can either overwhelm us, or make our lives better and our country stronger. What we can't do is pretend it is not happening. I hear people say we have to stop and debate globalisation. You might as well debate whether autumn
10 should follow summer. They're not debating it in China and India. They are seizing its possibilities, in a way that will transform their lives and ours. Yes, both nations still have millions living in poverty. But they are on the move. [...]
In the era of rapid globalisation, there is no mystery about what
15 works: an open, liberal economy, prepared constantly to change to remain competitive. The new world rewards those who are open to it. Foreign investment improves our economy. Or take immigration. We know we need strict controls. They are being put in place, along with Identity Cards, also necessary in a
20 changing world. But one of the most satisfying things about the election was that the country saw through the Tories nasty, unprincipled campaign on immigration. People who come to work and make their lives here make Britain not weaker but stronger. But there is a lesson here too. The temptation is to use
25 Government to try to protect ourselves against the onslaught of globalisation by shutting it out; to think we protect a workforce by regulation; a company by Government subsidy; an industry by tariffs. It doesn't work today. Because the dam holding back the global economy burst years ago. The compe-
30 tition can't be shut out, it can only be beaten. And the greatest error progressive politics can make, is, to think that somehow this more open and liberal world makes our values redundant, that the choice is either to cling onto the European social model of the past; or be helpless, swept along by the flow. On the
35 contrary, social solidarity remains the only way to secure the future of a country like Britain.
However, today its purpose is not to resist the force of globalisation but to prepare for it, and to garner its vast potential benefits. [...]
40 We know what makes a good school. Good leadership; great teachers; strong discipline; a love of learning. We know what makes good healthcare. Quick access; committed care; clean, comfortable surroundings. But what happens if you can't get them? If you've the money, you buy better. That is an affront
45 to every progressive value we believe in. There's a great myth

to seize to take hold of sth suddenly and violently

onslaught a strong or violent attack

subsidy money that is paid by a government or organization to make prices lower, reduce the cost of producing goods, etc.
tariffs a tax on goods coming into a country or going out of a country

to garner to acquire through one's own efforts

here: which is that we don't have a market in services now. We do. It's called private schools and private healthcare. But it's only open to the well-off. There is another myth: choice is a New Labour invention. Wrong. Choice is what wealthy people have exercised for centuries. The Tories have always 5 been comfortable with that. But for Labour choice is too important to be the monopoly of the wealthy. A final myth: the way to keep universal services universal is to make them uniform. Again, wrong. The way to keep services universal is to make them of such quality that enough of those who can af- 10 ford to go private, opt to stay in the public service. I will never return us to selection aged 11 in our schools. I will never allow the NHS to charge for treatment. [...]

Participation

Arthur Scargill: Fight for the future (1984)

Arthur Scargill delivered this speech during an extraordinary conference of the National Union of Miners in Sheffield during the time of the great strike (1984/1985).

[...] This Extraordinary Annual Conference takes place during the eighteenth week of the most, bitter dispute seen in the mining industry since 1926 – a strike sparked off by the Coal Board's announcement on March 6th that it intended to close 20 pits and destroy 20,000 jobs over the coming year alone, 5 as part of what Ian MacGregor termed "bringing supply into line with demand".

It was obvious that this decision marked the beginning of the pit closure programme announced by the Coal Board Chairman at a Consultative Council meeting over a year ago. On 10 June 14th, 1983 he declared it was the Board's intention to take 25 million tonnes of capacity out of the industry with the advent of the Selby coalfield. Translated into flesh and blood terms, this meant over 70 pit closures and 70,000 job losses.

By the time the Union presented its claim for wages in 1983, 15 it had become clear that the Board's intention was to run down the industry, getting rid of what it termed "uneconomic capacity".

Coal Board created in 1947 by Clement Attlee's government that nationalised industries

Ian MacGregor (1912–1998), referred to as the "butcher of the coal industry" by Scargill, became chairman of British Steel in 1979.

Selby town in North Yorkshire

This programme for butchering coal was strikingly similar to the industrial vandalism inflicted on the British steel industry, where Ian MacGregor wiped out over 100,000 jobs, and, earlier, at British Leyland where (in collaboration with Sir
5 Michael Edwardes) he destroyed a similar amount of jobs.
The policy now openly pursued by the National Coal Board utterly violates the Plan For Coal, agreed between Government, Coal Board and mining Unions in 1974, reaffirmed in 1977 and, more significantly, accepted by the present Gov-
10 ernment in 1979 and as recently as 1981. Delegates will not need reminding that our Union has consistently pledged itself to fight against pit closures and reductions in manpower levels, while at the same time demanding decent wages and conditions for British miners. We do not need reminding of
15 what took place in the 1960s when, in an era of what can only be described as collaboration, the Union acquiesced to a policy of mass destruction of jobs, pits and mining communities. We vowed that never again would we stand by and witness such vandalism – never again would we sit back and
20 watch our people turned into industrial gypsies, wandering from coalfield to coalfield, from pit to pit, searching for work: victims of the narrow, balance-sheet mentality of both Coal Board and Government.
Today, the devastation threatening our communities is dra-
25 matically and tragically compounded by the destructive monetarist policies which this Government has unleashed. With over four-and-a-half million unemployed people, Britain's industrial base crippled by lack of investment, and the nation's social services network being torn to shreds, there is
30 a climate of helplessness, hopelessness and outright despair. It is our responsibility as trade unionists to fight that despair and oppose the policies which created it.
When I was elected President of this Union, by over 70 per cent of the votes cast, I was elected on a programme of total
35 opposition to pit closures and reductions in manpower – a programme demanding better wages and conditions, aimed at restoring the wages of miners to at least the level approved by Parliament itself following the dispute in 1974. [...]
From the start of this dispute – in fact, from the day our over-
40 time ban began last November – there has been a lot of talk, particularly from the media, about democracy. I have noted with interest that those who are most vociferous in attacking our Union, telling it what it should and should not do, are in fact the non-elected editors of newspapers, or non-elected
45 judges. [...]

British Leyland vehicle manufacturing company founded in 1968. In 1986 it was renamed as the Rover Group.

Sir Michael Edwardes (*1930) was appointed chief executive of British Leyland in 1977.

to acquiesce to do what sb else wants or allow sth to happen even though you do not really agree with it

monetarist sb who believes that the best way to manage a country's economy is for the government to control and limit the amount of money that is available
to tear to shreds to criticize sb very severely

vociferous offensively loud

Throughout the past eighteen weeks, with over 80 per cent of British miners out on strike fighting for the survival of our industry, our pits, jobs and communities, we have witnessed the sad sight of a small section of our members ignoring, or trying to ignore, the Union's fight for the future. 5

I want to say to all those men who are still at work: no matter what arguments you put forward, you cannot ignore the most important and precious trade union principle upon which the strength of our movement has been built. When workers are in dispute, you do not cross picket lines. 10

During the course of this strike, well over 4,000 of our members have been arrested. Nearly 2,000 have been injured – many of them very seriously. Two miners have been killed fighting for the right to work. Each of these facts alone should have convinced any trade unionist to stop work immediately 15 – and give their support to policies for which our members have been prepared to give their lives.

Miners on strike and their families are suffering intense hardship in this dispute, and I can only applaud their incredible determination and courage. 20

Not only have they faced deprivation and hunger – they have found themselves in the front line facing the most massive assault on civil liberties and human rights ever launched against trade unionists in this country.

On the picket lines, riot police in full battle gear, on horse- 25 back and on foot, accompanied by police dogs, have been unleashed in violent attacks upon our members. We have seen in our communities and villages a level of police harassment and intimidation which organised British trade unionists have never before experienced. [...] 30

I appeal to those who are still at work: search your conscience. No trade unionist can justify crossing an official picket line. No trade union official can condone or collude in such an action. Look instead at the reasons why your colleagues are out on strike. They are fighting for your future and that of 35 your families as well as for their own.

picket line a group of people who stand outside a factory and try to prevent people from going in or coming out during a strike

deprivation the lack of sth that you need in order to be healthy, comfortable, or happy

to condone to accept or forgive behaviour that most people think is morally wrong
to collude to work with sb secretly, esp. in order to do sth dishonest or illegal

Margaret Thatcher: The strike is over (1985)

Margaret Thatcher gave this speech on March 23, 1985 in New-castle. She talked about the end of the strike and the positive developments her government had instigated for Britain.

Mr. Chairman, it has been an eventful year since the Central Council last met in Birmingham. For almost the whole of that time, the country lived through a coal strike. Yes, it cost us dear. But nothing like the price we would have paid had
5 we given in to violence and intimidation. The coal strike has cost the industry a year. The striking miners have gone a year without pay. The customers of coal have gone a year without their proper supplies.
Companies selling machinery to the Coal Board have seen
10 their order books halved. Strikes kill jobs inside and outside the mining industry.
Nevertheless, good offer after good offer was rejected by a ruthless leadership without a ballot. Mr. Chairman, the strike is over. This dark shadow has passed from our industrial land-
15 scape. The end of the strike should mark a historic watershed. All those working miners who walked across picket lines to a barrage of abuse and stones were walking purposefully to-wards the future – a future in which their views counted.
Through their courage, they showed the way forward; the
20 values of freedom and democracy are flourishing today in Britain. These are the things they cherish, Mr. Chairman, so do we.
In the coal industry and elsewhere in our industrial heart-lands, we have to move away from the old class-based con-
25 flict towards new styles of management.
If we act with a sense of common purpose; if we think of managers as workers, and of workers as potential owners, then we can create prosperous industry out of the barren lands of our old industrial areas.
30 Mr. Chairman, the coal strike may have dominated last year's news. But we should not allow it to obscure what we have achieved. The economy is producing more than ever before. Living standards are at an all-time high. Investment has hit new records. That is the sign of a fundamentally strong econ-
35 omy.
Before our time in Government, the conventional wisdom had been – don't try and reform the trade unions, they're too powerful. Well, that's precisely why we did reform them.

National Coal Board (NCB) created in 1947 by Clement Attlee's government as part of their programme for nationalising industries

ballot a system of voting, usually in secret
watershed an important point of transition

barrage a lot of criticisms, questions, complaints, etc. that come all at once, or very quickly one after another

to denationalise to sell off a business or industry that was previously owned by the state to private ownership

Sir Keith Joseph (1918–1995) was a member of Thatcher's Cabinet who had large impact on Thatcherism.

Our reforms changed attitudes. No longer could trade unions behave as if they were above the law. It used to be the conventional wisdom that we couldn't denationalise any State-owned companies. Not any more. Privatisation is popular. In the last year alone, we have denationalised Jaguar, Sealink 5 and British Telecom to name just a few. And there are more to come. Our achievements go wider than this. Thanks to Keith Joseph, we are raising standards in our schools. It is not all a question of money. But we don't say often enough that we are spending more on every pupil and have the best ever 10 teacher-pupil ratio.

It's a similar story in the National Health Service – more resources than ever before; far more than any Labour Government. And so the NHS can now treat a record number of patients.   15

And we've always kept faith with the pensioner. Their pensions too have record buying power.

But you will say – we accept that you have done all of this. But what about jobs? So yes, what about jobs? How are they created?   20

Socialists often start by distributing wealth. They forget it first has to be created.

You only provide new jobs if you generate more wealth and build up more businesses. It's Government's task to see that the citizen is not overtaxed, not overregulated, not overgov- 25 erned. Then private enterprise can get on with the rest.

Yet there is a consistent tendency in our society to downgrade the creators of wealth. And nowhere is this attitude more marked than in cloister and common-room. What these critics apparently can't stomach is that wealth-creators 30 have a tendency to acquire wealth in the process of creating it for others!

cloister *Kreuzgang (Kloster)*
common-room a room in a school or college that a group of teachers or students use to relax in
to stomach to tolerate or bear

enterprise the activity of starting and running businesses
vigour physical or mental energy and determination

But the truth is, Mr. Chairman, that the creation of wealth is the most fundamental of all social services. For it is the wealth-creator alone who has the enterprise, the resources 35 and the vigour to build the business which will put the unemployed back into work.

When I was in Washington recently, they told me that 20 million jobs had been created in the last fifteen years. And that nine out of every ten had come from companies em- 40 ploying less than one hundred people. Note – the jobs were not created by Government (they stressed that) – but by private enterprise

That is the message we have to get across here in Britain. Mr. Chairman, it's not always easy. Indeed, you may have no- 45

ticed that recently the voices of some [Rt. Rev. David Jenkins, Bishop of Durham] reverend and Rt. reverend prelates have been heard in the land. I make no complaint about that. After all, it wouldn't be Spring, would it, without the voice of
5 the occasional cuckoo! You may have noticed, too, that these clerical voices have been ranging fairly confidently into the sphere of economic management with their, quite detailed, advice. Well, perhaps I may venture to refer to the parable of the talents. Those who traded with their talents, and multi-
10 plied them, were those who won approval. And the essence of their performance was the willingness to take risks to make a gain.

That spirit of risk-taking and enterprise is back today. No government in years has made enterprise so worthwhile as the
15 present one.

Contrast what we have done with what the Labour Party want to do. They are now pledged to push income tax right back to where it was before we started bringing it down. And you remember what the top rate was then. It was 98 per cent.
20 That's not taxation. That's confiscation.

Wherever men or women with talents forgather today – in Boardrooms, or common-rooms, in clubs, or parishes – the real moral challenge should be: what opportunities are there or what opportunities have I missed, to launch some new,
25 profitable business, and to offer a job to the jobless in the process? The challenge is open to all.

With capitalism and free-enterprise, there are no boundaries of class or creed or colour. Everyone can climb the ladder as high as their talents will take them.
30 Some of our finest companies were started by people who came from modest backgrounds, or who fled to Britain from foreign oppression. They didn't speak with Oxford accents. They hadn't got what people call "the right connections". They had just one thing in common. They were men of action.
35 And what was their driving force? They wanted to build a business. They wanted to demonstrate to the world their success. They wanted to be independent, rather than depending on others. They were ambitious to make money – yes and what's wrong with that? – to give their children a better start
40 in life than they'd had.

Success earned through individual effort; sturdy independence – these are the virtues which we Conservatives applaud. And, Mr. Chairman, these are the virtues which create jobs for others – thousands, and thousands, and thousands of
45 jobs. [...]

Rt.Rev. Right Reverend

David Jenkins (*1925) was Bishop of Durham from 1984–1994 and an outspoken critic of Margaret Thatcher.

confiscation here: the seizing of private property for government use and without compensation
to forgather to meet in a group

creed a set of beliefs or principles

sturdy determined and not easily persuaded to change one's opinions

Britain and Europe

Tony Benn: I cannot hand away powers lent to me (1991)

Tony Benn, a populist of the left and more or less an anarchist, delivered this speech in the House of Commons on November 20, 1991. He consistently warned against Britain's joining the European Community, especially towards the end of 1991 when other European countries were preparing to sign the Maastricht treaty.

Jacques Delors (*1925) French economist and politician who served two terms as president of the European Commission (1985–1995)

sovereign 1. a king or queen; 2. a British gold coin used in the past

Margarita Papandreou wife of former Greek Socialist Prime Minister Andreas Papandreou; active in various feminist groups

Margaret Thatcher (*1925) Prime Minister of Britain from 1979–1990

Front Benches the front row of seats on each side of the British parliament that the leaders of the political parties sit on

people of Chesterfield Tony Benn's constituents
constituent a voter in a district represented by an elected official
crèche Krippe

Some people genuinely believe that we shall never get social justice from the British Government, but we shall get it from Jacques Delors. They believe that a good king is better than a bad Parliament. I have never taken that view. Others believe that change is inevitable, and that the common currency will ₅ protect us from inflation and will provide a wage policy. They believe that it will control speculation and that Britain cannot survive alone. None of those arguments persuade me because the argument has never been about sovereignty.
I do not know what a sovereign is apart from the one that ₁₀ used to be in gold and the Pope who is a sovereign in the Vatican. We are talking about democracy. No nation – not even the great United States which could, for all I know, be destroyed by a nuclear weapon from a third-world country – has the power to impose its will on other countries. We are ₁₅ discussing whether the British people are to be allowed to elect those who make the laws under which they are governed. The argument is nothing to do with whether we should get more maternity leave from Madame Papandreou than from Madame Thatcher. That is not the issue. ₂₀
I recognize that when the members of the three Front Benches agree, I am in a minority. My next job therefore is to explain to the people of Chesterfield what we have decided. I will say first, "My dear constituents, in future you will be governed by people whom you do not elect and cannot remove. I am ₂₅ sorry about it. They may give you better crèches and shorter working hours but you cannot remove them."
I know that it sounds negative but I have always thought it positive to say that the important thing about democracy is that we can remove without bloodshed the people who gov- ₃₀

ern us. We can get rid of a Callaghan, a Wilson or even a Right Hon. Lady by internal processes. We can get rid of the Right Hon. Member for Huntingdon. But that cannot be done in the structure that is proposed. Even if one likes the
5 policies of the people in Europe, one cannot get rid of them. Secondly, we say to my favourite friends, the Chartists and suffragettes, "All your struggles to get control of the ballot box were a waste of time. We shall be run in future by a few white persons, as in 1832." The instrument, I might add, is
10 the Royal Prerogative of treaty making. For the first time since 1649 the Crown makes the laws – advised, I admit, by the Prime Minister.

We must ask what will happen when people realize what we have done. We have had a marvellous debate about Europe,
15 but none of us has discussed our relationship with the people who sent us here. [...]

If people lose the power to sack their Government one of several things happens. First, people may just slope off. Apathy could destroy democracy. When the turnout drops below
20 50 per cent, we are in danger. [...]

The second thing that people can do is riot. Riot is an old-fashioned method for drawing the attention of the Government to what is wrong. It is difficult for an elected person to admit it, but the riot at Strangeways produced some prison
25 reforms. Riot has historically played a much larger part in British politics than we are ever allowed to know.

Thirdly, nationalism can arise. Instead of blaming the Treaty of Rome, people say, "It is those Germans" or "It is the French". Nationalism is built out of frustration that people
30 feel when they cannot get their way through the ballot box. With nationalism comes repression. I hope that it is not pessimistic – in my view it is not – to say that democracy hangs by a thread in every country in the world. Unless we can offer people a peaceful route to the resolution of injustices through
35 the ballot box, they will not listen to a House that has blocked off that route.

There are many alternatives open to us. One Hon. Member said that he was young and had not fought in the war. He looked at a new Europe. But there have been five Europes this
40 century. There was one run by the King, the Kaiser and the Tsar – they were all cousins so that was very comfortable. They were all Queen Victoria's grandsons. And there was no nonsense about human rights when Queen Victoria's grandsons repressed people. Then there was the Russian revolu-
45 tion. Then there was the inter-war period. Then there was the

---

Leonhard James ("Jim") Callaghan (1912–2005) Labour Prime Minister from 1976–1979

Harold Wilson (1916–1995) Labour Prime Minister from 1964–1970 and 1974–1976

Right Hon. Lady reference to Margaret Thatcher
Right Hon. Member for Huntingdon reference to Tony Blair

Chartist a working class mass movement for political and social reform that was active in the UK in the 1830s and 1840s

The **Reform Act of 1832** introduced changes to the electoral system of the UK.

Royal Prerogative rights and power available to a monarch
1649 Execution of King Charles I
turnout the number of people who vote in an election

Strangeways British prison where severe riots took place between April 1 – April 25, 1990

Treaty of Rome agreement signed by the leaders of six countries on 25 March, 1957 and which created the European Economic Community (EEC)

King, Kaiser, Tsar Queen Victoria's grandsons Wilhelm II (Germany), George V (Britain), Nicholas II (Russia)

Anglo-Soviet alliance. Then there was the cold war. Now we have Boris Yeltsin, who has joined the Monday Club. There have been many Europes. This is not the only Europe on offer. [...]

Another way would be to have a looser, wider Europe. I have an idea of a Commonwealth of Europe. I am introducing a bill on the subject. Europe would be rather like the British Commonwealth. We would work by consent with people. Or we could accept this ghastly proposal, which is clumsy, secretive, centralized, bureaucratic and divisive. That is how I regard the Treaty of Rome. I was born a European and I will die one. But I have never put my alliance behind the Treaty of Rome. I object to it. I hate being called an anti-European. How can one be anti-European when one is born in Europe? It is like saying that one is anti-British if one does not agree with the Chancellor of the Exchequer. What a lot of nonsense it is.

I ask myself why the House is ready to contemplate abandoning its duties, as I fear that it is. I was elected forty-one years ago this month. This Chamber has lost confidence in democracy. It believes that it must be governed by someone else. It is afraid to use the powers entrusted to it by its constituents. It has traded power for status. One gets asked to go on the telly if one is a Member of Parliament. The Chamber does not want to use its power. It has accepted the role of a spectator and joined what Bagehot called the dignified part of the constitution, leaving the Crown under the control of the Prime Minister, to be the Executive part.

If democracy is destroyed in Britain it will not be the communists, Trotskyists or subversives but this House which threw it away. The rights that are entrusted to us are not for us to give away. Even if I agree with everything that is proposed, I cannot hand away powers lent to me for five years by the people of Chesterfield. I just could not do it. It would be theft of public rights.

Therefore, there is only one answer. If people are determined to submit themselves to Jacques Delors, Madame Papandreaou and the Council of Ministers, we must tell the people what is planned. If people vote for that, they will all have capitulated. Julius Caesar said, "We are just merging our sovereignty." So did William the Conqueror.

It is not possible to support the Government's motion. I have told the Chief Whip that I cannot support the Labour motion. I invite the House to vote against the Government's motion and not to support a motion which purports to take us faster into a Community which cannot reflect the aspirations of those who put us here. That is not a nationalist argument nor is it about sovereignty. It is a democratic argument and it should be decisive in a democratic Chamber.

Douglas Alexander: Britain's place in today's European Union (2005)

On May 20, 2005, Douglas Alexander (Minister for Europe) delivered this speech in the Guildhall in London during a meeting of the Corporation of London. He declared his belief that Britain would gain advantages from her ties to the European Union.

Ladies and gentleman, it is a pleasure to speak to you here in the heart of the City of London about Britain and Europe. May I thank the officers and members of the Corporation of London for their generous hospitality today.
5 I have no doubt that, over the decades, these walls have heard the arguments for and against Europe on countless occasions. I have no doubt either that those who work within the Corporation of London and the City would have little hesitation in saying that Britain's membership of the EU over the past
10 thirty years has been one of the key factors in the City's success as the financial heart of Europe.
I come here today, as Minister for Europe, to put the case for a practical Europe which delivers real, practical benefits – jobs, security, a better quality of life for the citizens of Britain.
15 So, this morning I want to set out the practical benefits to Britain of our EU membership, the direction the EU now needs to take if it is to continue delivering those benefits and the role Britain could and should play in that reforming Europe. Thirty years ago, when Britain voted to continue our
20 membership of the European Economic Community, we did so out of self-interest. Continental Europe's economy was strong; Britain's was weak. Europe was the solution to Britain's problems as Roy Hattersley encapsulated, so succinctly in the House of Commons debate in 1971 when he said: 'I
25 regard the prospect of economic growth as the primary object or the principal prize of Europe. When I look back on the record of the government of which I was proud to be a member between 1964 and 1970, I have no doubt that we would have done a great deal better had we achieved the right

Roy Hattersley Deputy Leader of the Labour Party from 1983–1992

to encapsulate to express in a brief, but very fitting way

amount of economic growth. The housing targets would have been achieved; the school leaving age would have been raised; the National Health Service would have been financed differently; our overseas aid targets would have been met. I would vote for Europe if that were the only prospect that it 5 offers – but it is not'. Roy recognised the economic benefits that joining the European Union would bring, but he also echoed a case originally made by the founders of the European idea like Churchill and Jean Monnet and by the most prominent pro-Europeans in Britain like Ted Heath and Roy 10 Jenkins; a case based around peace, prosperity and democracy. Many pro-Europeans still point to that traditional case:

- Peace is not just about France and Germany, but preventing war and encouraging reconciliation across Europe, in particular in Central and Eastern Europe after 1989.   15

- Prosperity is not just about a free trade area – but a single market policed by a strong commission, and a voice for fair trade in the world that led to the creation of the WTO.

- Democracy is not just about Greece, Spain, Portugal and the miracle of a Europe whole and free. But the transformative 20 effect in the Balkans and in Turkey which scrapped the death penalty and introduced new laws to guarantee religious, cultural and media freedom, in the hope of joining the EU.

So in the twentieth century the case for Europe was based on contemporary circumstances of war, economic catch-up and 25 escape from the symptoms of the British disease. But today the position from which we view the future is fundamentally different. The UK is enjoying the longest period of sustained economic growth in its industrial history. And, above all, a stable economy achieved through monetary and fiscal disci- 30 pline which has given us the lowest interest rates for 40 years, the lowest inflation for 30 years and the highest employment levels in our history. Today we are the strongest large economy in Europe.

Growth in the UK economy is inextricably linked to our EU 35 membership. The proof that Europe has been good for Britain is all around us. Not only are more than 3 million jobs in the UK linked, directly or indirectly, to exports to the EU. But over half our trade is with the EU; 750,000 British-based companies trade across the EU and the Single Market, alone, has 40 generated a further £20 billion for the UK economy.

Our contemporary views, however, should reflect the fact that

---

Winston Churchill (1874–1965) British Prime Minister from 1940–1945 and 1951–1955 (cf. p. 98)

Jean Monnet (1888–1979) French economist and politician regarded by many as the architect of the European Community

Ted Heath (1916–2005) British Prime Minister from 1970–1974

Roy Jenkins (1920–2003) British Labour politician who was one of the founders of the Social Democratic Party in 1981

WTO World Trade Organisation, founded in 1994

to scrap to decide not to use a plan or system because it is not practical

monetary relating to money, esp all the money in a particular country

inextricable unable to be separated

the EU of which we are part today is quite different from the
one we joined over 30 years ago. In all the discussions about
Brussels and the EU Constitutional Treaty, few commentators
have noticed quite how different an expanded Europe of 25
5 actually is – and how the injection of 10 new members has
changed the nature of debates within it. The dynamic of the
expanded European Union today is towards liberalisation not
harmonisation, expansion not integration.

And these trends reflect the fact that Europe, itself, is facing a
10 new and very different world. I bring to this job, as Europe
Minister, the perspective and understanding gained as Trade
Minister. Europe needs to adapt to the changing balance of
global economic activity and the rise of fast-growing economies, notably China and India which, respectively, aspire to
15 be the global manufacturing and services hub of the 21st century global economy.

So while Europe has successfully responded to the challenge
of history through internal reform, in an age of globalisation
Europe must now build on the historic achievement of en-
20 largement by meeting the challenges of the future by looking
outwards. Rapid technological change, global capital flows
and the global sourcing of products are leading to an increasingly competitive global market for goods, services and investment. The most successful economies will be those that
25 can adapt quickly to change, promote entrepreneurship and
innovation, and move up the value chain.

That is why, under the British Presidency starting on July 1st,
we will make a priority of advancing the economic reform
agenda. Let me give just 3 examples:

30 We will take action to help business by advancing the better
regulation agenda. First, improving the policy-making process by better consultation and Impact Assessments which
should include measuring the burden on business and testing the impact on the EU's international competitiveness.
35 Second, reducing the volume and complexity of EU legislation. Third, reviewing the impact and outcomes of existing
legislation. [...]

Finally we will take action to strengthen EU/US economic cooperation. We will want to build on the June EU/US Summit
40 and demonstrate clear progress in breaking down barriers to
trade and investment in priority areas.

Around such measures I want to work with business and
across Party lines to forge a pro-reform, pro-Europe consensus. I believe Europe can now develop the tools and confi-
45 dence to look outwards and tackle globalisation just as, in

EU Constitutional Treaty
Treaty establishing a constitution for the European
Community. It was signed by
representatives of all member states in 2004, but the
referendum was rejected by
the populations of France
and the Netherlands in 2005.

hub centre

past decades, it has tackled war and instability on the European continent.

For what, in fact, unites many of those across Europe, opposed to the new Constitutional Treaty, with many of the sceptics here in the United Kingdom, is their lack of confi- 5 dence in the future.

The sceptics argue that the very existence of Europe threatens our sense of identity. Britain's historical ambivalence about continental entanglement has, undoubtedly, been central to debates about Europe. But this story of Britain against Eu- 10 rope, of 'splendid isolation', seen through the prism of 'our finest hour' – Waterloo, the Armada and Agincourt – tells only part of the story. Behind the focus on the 'Blue water' history of British empire, is a story of deep engagement in European history over millennia.   15

It is uncomfortable for many of today's sceptics to acknowledge that even Margaret Thatcher, at the height of her powers, was clear that Britain's destiny lay in Europe. In her speech to the College of Europe in Bruges in 1988 she spoke of the '2000 years of British involvement in Europe, co- 20 operation with Europe and contribution to Europe, a contribution which is today as valid and as strong as ever'.

I believe sincerely that, after more than thirty years, Britain's sense of its own identity has not been undermined by membership of the EU. National identities, reflecting distinctive 25 history, language and cultural values forged over hundreds of years, are far more resilient than that.

To be sure, the European Union, has not, at times, helped itself over the years by allowing some of its critics to suggest that its aspirations are to ape the trappings of a nation state 30 with symbols such as flags and anthems. But we should be clear that those trappings are just that. The EU – as defined by the Constitutional Treaty – is not designed to submerge the nation state and deny national identity, but instead is a unique organisation by which nation states have worked ef- 35 fectively together to enhance their power and influence.

And when the wall came down in 1989, the countries of Central and Eastern Europe recognized that too. As they threw off the yoke of Soviet occupation they turned to the EU as part of the process of rediscovering their national identities 40 and asserting their independence. So, being in favour of Europe today does not, and should not, mean denying the need for change and reform where change and reform are needed. Instead our vision of a reformed Europe is one that allows Britain to walk tall in the emerging age of globalisation. Over 45

splendid isolation term for the foreign policy pursued by late 19th century Britain under the conservative Prime Minister Benjamin Disraeli

Waterloo The Battle of Waterloo on 18 June, 1815 led to the final defeat of Napoleon Bonaparte.

Armada Spanish fleet sent by Philip II in 1588 that was defeated by England

Agincourt The Battle of Agincourt was fought on 25 October 1415 during the Hundred Years' War. Henry V defeated the French.

Margaret Thatcher (*1925) Conservative Prime Minister from 1979 to 1990 (cf. p. 66)

Bruges *Brügge*
resilient *unverwüstlich*
to ape to copy sb's way of doing sth, without thinking about it just as a monkey would

yoke sth that restricts one's freedom

the past 8 years we have experienced growing influence: setting the agenda for European defence at St Malo; taking a
lead on economic reform at Lisbon; helping Europe deal with
organised crime at Tampere. Negotiating a constitution that
5 had so much of our agenda that the French Eurosceptics call
it 'la constitution britannique'. But we have also known what
it is like to be isolated and marginalised, seeing Europe as
something that is done to us, rather than a vehicle to have an
influence in a globalised world.
10 Now we have a choice to make. On the one hand, we have a
Treaty that can help us realise our vision of more power to
the member states, through the European Council, where national governments set the EU's priorities and ensure that
they can be carried through. The current system of six-month
15 rotating presidencies of the European Council will be re-
placed by a fulltime Chair to ensure that it is we, the nations,
who set the EU's agenda and get it implemented. [...]

St Malo walled port city in
Brittany, site of an Anglo-
French summit in 1998 that
was highly important for
European defence strategy

Lisbon capital of Portugal,
site of the Spring European
council in march 2000 at
which European leaders
agreed to a 10-year strategy
of economic reforms for
Europe

Tampere city in southern
Finland, site of a special
meeting of the European
Council to consider such
issues as freedom, security,
justice and immigration

Biographies

Queen Elizabeth II (*1926) started studying Constitutional History and Law when in 1936 it became apparent that she would become queen. In 1947, she married Philip Mountbatten, and together, they had four children. When her father, King George VI, died in 1952 she became Queen Elizabeth II.

Michael Portillo (*1953) had a Spanish father who had fled Spain at the end of the civil war. In the General Election in 1979, he was adviser to Margaret Thatcher. He was then a member of the government from 1986–1997. After his electoral defeat in 1997, he turned to journalism, working for *The Scotsman* and the BBC.

Tony Blair (*1953): At just 30 years of age, Tony Blair won a seat in the 1983 General Election. In 1997, he led the Labour Party to a landslide victory in the General Election after 18 years in Opposition. This meant that, at the age of 43, Tony Blair became one of the youngest Prime Ministers in the history of Great Britain. He stepped back from office in June 2007.

Arthur Scargill (*1938) became president of the National Union of Mineworkers in 1981. He is best known for his strong Socialist defence of British miners both during the Great Strike (1984/85) and when British Coal announced the closure of most deep-mine colliers in 1992.

Margaret Thatcher (*1925) was the UK's first female prime minister. Thatcher favoured privatisation plans and led Britain through the Falklands War with Argentina. Because of her uncompromising attitude, she was often called "The Iron Lady". She was eventually forced to resign in 1990.

Tony Benn (*1925) joined the Labour Party in 1942 and retired in 2001 after fifty years in Parliament. During his career he served as a Cabinet minister in both the Wilson and Callaghan governments (1964–1979), published a series of diaries in seven volumes and has written several other books.

Douglas Alexander (*1967) studied Politics and Modern History at the Lester B. Pearson College in Vancouver, the University of Edinburgh and the University of Pennsylvania, and in 1993, qualified as a solicitor. Having joined the Labour Party while still at school in 1982, he first became a Member of Parliament in 1997, and has served in different posts in Tony Blair's Cabinet ever since.

IV. Postcolonial times

India

Mahatma Gandhi: Quit India (1942)

Mahatma Gandhi delivered this speech in an address to the Indian Congress urging the British to grant India independence.

The **resolution** discussed here demanded full independence for all of India and its 90 million inhabitants.

to approve of to think that sth/sb is good or acceptable
to enjoin to order sb to do sth

utterance sth you say, statement

Ahimsa (*Sanskrit*) absolute non-violence

contemplated deeply thought about

wearied of no longer interested in

to vouchsafe to give sb sth as a privilege

Himsa (*Sanskrit*) absolute violence
deliverance the state of being rescued from danger

Before you discuss the resolution, let me place before you one or two things, I want you to understand two things very clearly and to consider them from the same point of view from which I am placing them before you. I ask you to consider it from my point of view, because if you approve of it, 5 you will be enjoined to carry out all I say. It will be a great responsibility. There are people who ask me whether I am the same man that I was in 1920, or whether there has been any change in me. You are right in asking that question.

Let me, however, hasten to assure that I am the same Gandhi 10 as I was in 1920. I have not changed in any fundamental respect. I attach the same importance to non-violence that I did then. If at all, my emphasis on it has grown stronger. There is no real contradiction between the present resolution and my previous writings and utterances. 15

Occasions like the present do not occur in everybody's and but rarely in anybody's life. I want you to know and feel that there is nothing but purest Ahimsa in all that I am saying and doing today. The draft resolution of the Working Committee is based on Ahimsa, the contemplated struggle similarly has 20 its roots in Ahimsa. If, therefore, there is any among you who has lost faith in Ahimsa or is wearied of it, let him not vote for this resolution.

Let me explain my position clearly. God has vouchsafed to me a priceless gift in the weapon of Ahimsa. I and my Ahim- 25 sa are on our trail today. If in the present crisis, when the earth is being scorched by the flames of Himsa and crying for deliverance, I failed to make use of the God given talent, God will not forgive me and I shall be judged unwrongly of the great gift. I must act now. I may not hesitate and merely look on, when Russia and China are threatened.

Ours is not a drive for power, but purely a non-violent fight for India's independence. In a violent struggle, a successful
5 general has been often known to effect a military coup and to set up a dictatorship. But under the Congress scheme of things, essentially non-violent as it is, there can be no room for dictatorship. A non-violent soldier of freedom will covet nothing for himself, he fights only for the freedom of his
10 country. The Congress is unconcerned as to who will rule, when freedom is attained. The power, when it comes, will belong to the people of India, and it will be for them to decide to whom it is placed and entrusted. May be that the reins will be placed in the hands of the Parsis, for instance –
15 as I would love to see happen – or they may be handed to some others whose names are not heard in the Congress today. It will not be for you then to object saying, "This community is microscopic. That party did not play its due part in the freedom's struggle; why should it have all the power?"
20 Ever since its inception the Congress has kept itself meticulously free of the communal taint. It has thought always in terms of the whole nation and has acted accordingly [...]

I know how imperfect our Ahimsa is and how far away we are still from the ideal, but in Ahimsa there is no final failure or
25 defeat. I have faith, therefore, that if, in spite of our shortcomings, the big thing does happen, it will be because God wanted to help us by crowning with success our silent, unremitting Sadhana for the last twenty-two years.

I believe that in the history of the world, there has not been
30 a more genuinely democratic struggle for freedom than ours. I read Carlyle's French Revolution while I was in prison, and Pandit Jawaharlal has told me something about the Russian revolution. But it is my conviction that inasmuch as these struggles were fought with the weapon of violence they failed
35 to realize the democratic ideal. In the democracy which I have envisaged, a democracy established by non-violence, there will be equal freedom for all. Everybody will be his own master. It is to join a struggle for such democracy that I invite you today. Once you realize this you will forget the differ-
40 ences between the Hindus and Muslims, and think of yourselves as Indians only, engaged in the common struggle for independence.

Then, there is the question of your attitude towards the British. I have noticed that there is hatred towards the British
45 among the people. The people say they are disgusted with

to covet to want sth very much, esp. sth belonging to sb else

rein long, thin leather band used to control a horse; here: the control of the country
Parsi small, yet united, religious community in India

inception start of an institution/organization
meticulous very careful
taint a trace of sth bad or immoral

unremitting persistent, never-ending
Sadhana (*Sanskrit*) means of attainment, building of willpower and confidence in yourself and God

Thomas Carlyle (1795–1888) writer and historian, wrote three books about the French Revolution

Pandit Jawaharlal better known as Nehru (1889–1964). At the Congress of Oppressed Nationalities in Brussels (1927), Nehru was elected to a nine-member executive committee along with Romain Rolland, Madame Sun Yat Sen and Albert Einstein.

their behaviour. The people make no distinction between British imperialism and the British people. To them, the two are one. This hatred would even make them welcome the Japanese. It is most dangerous. It means that they will exchange one slavery for another. We must get rid of this feel- 5 ing. Our quarrel is not with the British people, we fight their imperialism. The proposal for the withdrawal of British power did not come out of anger. It came to enable India to play its due part at the present critical juncture. It is not a happy position for a big country like India to be merely helping 10 with money and material obtained willy-nilly from her while the United Nations are conducting the war. We cannot evoke the true spirit of sacrifice and valour, so long as we are not free. I know the British Government will not be able to withhold freedom from us, when we have made enough self-sac- 15 rifice. We must, therefore, purge ourselves of hatred. Speaking for myself, I can say that I have never felt any hatred. As a matter of fact, I feel myself to be a greater friend of the British now than ever before. One reason is that they are today in distress. My very friendship, therefore, demands that I 20 should try to save them from their mistakes. As I view the situation, they are on the brink of an abyss. It, therefore, becomes my duty to warn them of their danger even though it may, for the time being, anger them to the point of cutting off the friendly hand that is stretched out to help them. 25 People may laugh, nevertheless that is my claim. At a time when I may have to launch the biggest struggle of my life, I may not harbour hatred against anybody.

willy-nilly whether you want to or not

valour great courage

to purge to rid oneself of sth impure

the brink of an abyss the edge of a very deep hole

Clement Attlee: The end of British rule in India (1947)

Labour Prime minister Attlee granted India independence and announced this decision in British parliament on February 20, 1947.

I desire to make a statement on Indian policy.

It has long been the policy of successive British governments to work toward the realization of self-government in India. In pursuance of this policy, an increasing measure of respon-

pursuance (*fml*) following, carrying out an activity

sibility has been devolved on Indians and today the civil administration and the Indian Armed Forces rely to a very large extent on Indian civilians and officers. In the constitutional field, the Acts of 1919 and 1935 passed by the British Parliament each represented a substantial transfer of political power. In 1940 the Coalition Government recognized the principle that Indians should themselves frame a new constitution for a fully autonomous India, and in the offer of 1942, they invited them to set up a Constituent Assembly for this purpose as soon as the war was over.

His Majesty's government believe this policy to have been right and in accordance with sound democratic principles. Since they came into office, they have done their utmost to carry it forward to its fulfilment. The declaration of the prime minister of 15ᵗʰ March last, which met with general approval in Parliament and the country, made it clear that it was for the Indian people themselves to choose their future status and constitution and that, in the opinion of His Majesty's government, the time had come for responsibility for the government of India to pass into Indian hands. […]

It is with great regret that His Majesty's government find that there are still differences among Indian parties which are preventing the Constituent Assembly from functioning as it was intended that it should. It is of the essence of the plan that the Assembly should be fully representative.

His Majesty's government desire to hand over responsibility to authorities established by a constitution approved by all parties in India in accordance with the Cabinet Mission's plan, but unfortunately, there is at present, no clear prospect that such a constitution and such authorities will emerge. The present state of uncertainty is fraught with danger and cannot be indefinitely prolonged. His Majesty's government wish to make it clear that it is their definite intention to take the necessary steps to effect the transference of power into Indian hands by a date not later than June 1948.

This great sub-continent now containing over 400 million people has, for the last century, enjoyed peace and security as a part of the British Commonwealth and Empire.

Continued peace and security are more than ever necessary today if the full possibilities of economic development are to be realized and a higher standard of life attained by the Indian people.

His Majesty's government are anxious to hand over their responsibilities to a government which, resting on the sure foundation of the support of the people, is capable of main-

to devolve (*fml*) to pass on power to a person at a lower level

fraught with full of

to attain (*fml*) to succeed in achieving sth after trying for a long time

taining peace and administering India with justice and efficiency. It is therefore essential that all parties should sink
their differences in order that they be ready to shoulder the
great responsibilities which will come to them next year. [...]
His Majesty's government believe that British commercial 5
and industrial interests in India can look forward to a fair
field for their enterprise under the new conditions. The commercial connection between India and the United Kingdom
has been long and friendly, and will continue to be to their
mutual advantage. 10
His Majesty's government cannot conclude this statement
without expressing on behalf of the people of this country
their goodwill and the good wishes toward the people of India as they go forward to this final stage in their achievement
of self-government. It will be the wish of everyone in these 15
notwithstanding despite, in spite of   islands that, notwithstanding constitutional changes, the association of the British and Indian peoples should not be
brought to an end, and they will wish to continue to do all
that is in their power to further the well-being of India.

Winston Churchill: Britain's shameful flight from India (1947)

On March 6, 1947, two weeks after Clement Attlee's speech (cf.
pp. 70ff.), Winston Churchill, former Prime Minister and then
leader of the Conservative opposition, made this speech in response to the policy of Labour government toward India.

When great parties in this country have for so many years
to pursue to continue doing or trying to achieve   pursued a combined and united policy on some large issue,
and when, for what seemed to them to be good reasons, they
decide to separate, not only in debate but by division, it is
desirable and even necessary that the causes of such separa- 5
tion and the limitations of the differences which exist should
be placed on record. This afternoon we begin a new chapter
in our relations across the floor of the House in regard to the
Indian problem. We on this side of the House have, for some
time, made it clear that the sole responsibility for the control 10
of India's affairs rests, of course, with His Majesty's government. We have criticized their actions in various ways but
this is the first time we have felt it our duty as the official Op-
dissent disagreement   position to express our dissent by a formal vote.

Let us first place on record the measure of agreement which lies between us, and separate that from the differences that now lead us into opposite lobbies. Both sides of the House are bound by the declaration made at the time of the British mis-
5 sion to India in March 1942. It is not true to suggest, as was done lately, that this decision marked a decisive change in the policy of the British Parliament toward India. There was a long story before we got to that. Great Britain had for many years been committed to handing over responsibility for the
10 government of India to the representatives of the Indian people. There was the promise of dominion status implicit in the declaration of August, 1917. There was the expansion and definition of dominion status by the Statute of Westminster. There was the Simon Commission Report of 1930, followed
15 by the Hoare-Linlithgow Reforms of 1935. There was the Linlithgow offer of 1940, for which, as head of the government in those days, I took my share of responsibility. By this, the viceroy undertook that, as soon as possible after the war, Indians themselves should frame a fully self-governing constitu-
20 tion. All this constituted the preliminary basis on which the proposals of the Cripps Mission of 1942 were set. The proposals of this mission were not, in fact, a departure in principle from what had long been growing up, but they constituted a definite, decisive and urgent project for action. Let us con-
25 sider the circumstances in which this offer was made.

The violent eruption of Japan upon East Asia, the withdrawal of the United States fleet to the American coast, the sinking of the Prince of Wales and the Repulse, the loss of Malaya and the surrender of Singapore, and many other circumstances of
30 that time left us for the moment without any assured means of defending India from invasion by Japan. We had lost the command of the Bay of Bengal, and, indeed, to a large extent, of the Indian Ocean. Whether the provinces of Madras and Bengal would be pillaged and ravaged by the Japanese at the
35 time seemed to hang in the balance, and the question naturally arose with poignant force how best to rally all Indian elements to the defense of their native land.

The offer of the Cripps Mission, I would remind the House, was substantially this: His Majesty's government undertook
40 to accept and implement an agreed constitution for an Indian Union, which should be a dominion, framed by an elected Constituent Assembly and affording representation to the princes. This undertaking was subject only to the right of non-acceding provinces to receive separate treatment, and to
45 the conclusion of a treaty guaranteeing the protection of all

---

dominion status self-governing country belonging to the British Empire or Commonwealth

Statute of Westminster act of Parliament passed in 1931 establishing legislative equality between self-governing dominions of the Empire and the United Kingdom

Simon Commission a group of 7 British MPs sent to India in 1927 to study constitutional reform in India and produce a report on it

viceroy *Vizekönig*

assured confident about your own abilities

to pillage to steal things by force, esp. during a war; plunder

poignant here: pressing, relevant to the moment

non-acceding not agreeing

vocal expressing strongly
disagreeing opinions

**National Coalition
Government** i.e. Churchill's
wartime government

present prime minister
i.e. Clement Attlee

to repudiate to refuse to
accept

to discharge here: to get rid of
an obligation
hon. honourable

stipulation (*fml*) sth that must
be done, part of an agreement

to subordinate to put sb or
sth in a less important position

religious and racial minorities. The offer of the Cripps Mission
was not accepted by the political classes of India who alone
are vocal and to whom it was addressed. On the contrary, the
Congress, led by Mr. Gandhi and Mr. Nehru, did their utmost
to make a revolt intended to paralyze the perilous communi- 5
cations of our Army in Burma and to help the fortunes of Japan. Therefore, the National Coalition Government of those
days made a large series of mass arrests of Indian Congress
leaders, and the bulk were kept in prison until the end of the
war. I was not myself present in the cabinet when these deci- 10
sions were taken. I was at Cairo preparing for the operations
which opened at Alamein, but I highly approved the action
which was taken in my absence by the then deputy prime
minister, the present prime minister, who sits opposite, and
which I think was the only one possible on that occasion.   15
Therefore, it is quite clear that, whatever was the offer of the
Cripps Mission, it was not accepted. On the contrary, it was
repudiated by the parties to whom it was addressed ... Both
sides of this House are bound by this offer, and bound by all
of it, and it is on the basis of this offer being an agreed matter 20
between the parties, and on that basis alone, that our present
and future controversies arise. If I am bound by the offer of
the dominion status and all that it implies, the prime minister is equally bound, or was equally bound, to the conditions
about agreement between the principal communities, about 25
the proper discharge of our pledges about the protection of
minorities and the like. The right hon. Gentleman has a perfect right to change his mind. He may cast away all these
stipulations which we jointly made, and proceed only with
the positive side of the offer. He has the right to claim the 30
support of his parliamentary majority for whatever action he
takes, but he has no right to claim our support beyond the
limits to which we are engaged by the Cripps declaration ...
I am only trying to lay down the basis on which we can agree
to differ – the basis of 1942 and the present time. Before this 35
latest pronouncement of theirs, His Majesty's government
had already departed from the Cripps Mission declaration of
1942, and they had departed from it in three major aspects.
First, they had eliminated the stage of dominion status. The
Cripps Mission expressly said that the objective was the crea- 40
tion of a new Indian Union which would constitute a dominion associated with the United Kingdom and the other dominions by common allegiance to the Crown, but equal to
them in every respect, in no way subordinated in any aspect
of domestic or external affairs ...   45

If the dominion status procedure had been involved, in my view, the new Indian Dominion would have been perfectly free to leave the Commonwealth if it chose, but full opportunity would have been given for all the dangers and disadvan-
5 tages to be surveyed by responsible Indian ministers beforehand, and also for the wishes of the great mass of the Indian people to be expressed, as they cannot be expressed right now. It would have been possible to insert into the dominion constitution the necessary safeguards for minorities, and for
10 the fulfillment of the British pledges to the various elements of Indian life, notably the depressed classes. This would have been a part of the agreement between the Indian Union and Great Britain, and would have been embodied in the necessary British legislation on the lines of the British North Amer-
15 ica Act, to which the great free Dominion of Canada has always attached importance, and still does. So the second departure of the Cripps Mission declaration was the total abandonment by His Majesty's government of all responsibility for carrying out its pledges to minorities and the de-
20 pressed classes, as well as for fulfilling their treaties with the Indian states. All these are to be left to fend for themselves, or to fight for themselves as best they can. That is a grave major departure.

The third departure was no less grave. The essence of the
25 Cripps Mission declaration was that there should be agreement between the principal Indian communities, namely, in fact, the Muslims and the Hindus. That, also, has been thrown overboard.

I do not think that the fourteen-months' time limit gives the
30 new viceroy a fair chance. We do not know what directives have been given to him. No explanation of that has been provided. Indeed, we are told very little. Looking on this Indian problem and having to address the House upon it, I am surprised how many great gaps there are in information
35 which should be in the full possession of the House. We are told very little. What is the policy and purpose for which he is to be sent out, and how is he to employ these fourteen months? Is he to make a new effort to restore the situation, or is it merely "Operation Scuttle" on which he and other
40 distinguished officers have been despatched? ...

Everyone knows that the fourteen-months' time limit is fatal to any orderly transference of power, and I am bound to say that the whole thing wears the aspect of an attempt by the government to make use of brilliant war figures in order to
45 cover up a melancholy and disastrous transaction. One thing

to fend for oneself to look after oneself

Operation Scuttle (*ironic*) scuttle = to move quickly with short steps because you are afraid

to despatch (also dispatch) (*fml*) to send sb somewhere for a particular reason

British Raj the rule of the British government in India from 1858 to 1947

clad wearing a particular kind of clothing

surge sudden movement of a lot of people

Created in 1885, the **Congress Party** became the force for Indian independence.

All India Muslim League was the driving force behind the creation of Pakistan as a Muslim country.

conscription when people are made to join the army
compulsion the act of forcing sb to do sth they do not want to do

tribulation (*fml*) serious trouble/problem

seems to me absolutely certain. The government, by their fourteen-months' time limit, have put an end to all prospect of Indian unity. I myself have never believed that that could be preserved after the departure of the British Raj, but the last chance has been extinguished by the government's action. 5
How can one suppose that the thousand-year gulf that yawns between Muslims and Hindus will be bridged in fourteen months? Here are these people, in many cases, of the same race, charming people, lightly clad, crowded together in all the streets and bazaars and so forth, and yet there is no inter- 10 marriage. It is astounding. Religion has raised a bar which not even the strongest impulse of nature can overleap. It is an astounding thing. Yet the government expect in fourteen months that there will be an agreement on these subjects between these races ... 15
Let the House remember this. The Indian political parties and political classes do not represent the Indian masses. It is a delusion to believe that they do. I wish they did. They are not as representative of them as the movements in Britain repre- sent the surges and impulses of the British nation. This has 20 been proved in the war, and I can show the House how it was proved. The Congress Party declared non-cooperation with Great Britain and the Allies. The other great political party to whom all main power is to be given, the Muslim League, sought to make a bargain about it, but no bargain was made. 25 So both great political parties in India, the only forces that have been dealt with so far, stood aside. Nevertheless, the only great volunteer army in the world that fought on either side in that struggle was formed in India. More than three and a half million men came forward to support the king- 30 emperor and the cause of Britain; they came forward not by conscription or compulsion, but out of their loyalty to Brit- ain and to all that Britain stood for in their lives. In handing over the government of India to these so-called political classes, we are handing over to men of straw, of whom, in a 35 few years, no trace will remain ...
We are told that we cannot walk out of Palestine because we should leave behind us a war between 600,000 Jews and 200,000 Arabs. How then can we walk out of India in four- teen months and leave behind us a war between 90 million 40 Muslims and 200 million Hindus, and all the other tribula- tions which will fall upon the helpless population of 400 million? Will it not be a terrible disgrace to our name and record if, after our fourteen-months' time limit, we allow one fifth of the population of the globe, occupying a region near- 45

ly as large as Europe, to fall into chaos and carnage? Would it not be a world crime that we should be committing, a crime that would stain – not merely strip us, as we are being stripped in the material position – but would stain our good name for
5 ever?

Yesterday, the president of the Board of Trade and other speakers brought into great prominence our physical and military weakness. How can we keep a large army in India for 15 or 20 years? He and other speakers stressed that point;
10 and, certainly, it is a very grave point. But he might as well have urged that in our present forlorn condition we have, not only not the physical strength, but not the moral strength and will power. If we, through lack of physical and moral strength, cannot wind up our affairs in a responsible and hu-
15 mane and honourable fashion, ought we not to consider invoking the aid or, at least, the advice of the world international organization, which is now clothed with reality, and on which so many of us, in all parts of the House, base our hopes for the peaceful progress, freedom and, indeed, the
20 salvation of all mankind? …

I thank the House for listening so long and so attentively to what I have said. I have spoken with a lifetime of thought and contact with these topics. It is with deep grief that I watch the clattering down of the British Empire, with all its
25 glories and all the services it has rendered to mankind. I am sure that in the hour of our victory, now not so long ago, we had the power, or could have had the power, to make a solution to our difficulties which could have been honourable and lasting. Many have defended Britain against her foes.
30 None can defend her against herself. We must face the evils that are coming upon us, and that we are powerless to avert. We must do our best in all these circumstances, and not exclude any expedient that may help to mitigate the ruin and disaster that will follow the disappearance of Britain from the
35 East. But, at least, let us not add – by shameful flight, by a premature, hurried scuttle – at least, let us not add, to the pangs of sorrow so many of us feel, the taint and smear of shame.

carnage the killing a lot of people all at once

Board of Trade Committee of the Privy Council of the UK, has been called the Department of Trade and Industry since 1970

expedient effective way of dealing with a problem

taint trace of sth bad or immoral

Jawaharlal Nehru: The granting of Indian independence (1947)

When in August 1947 independence was finally granted, Nehru made two speeches: the first to the Indian parliament, the second to the nation over the radio.

I.

tryst a secret meeting between lovers
to redeem a pledge to do what you have promised to do

Long years ago we made a tryst with destiny, and now the time comes when we shall redeem our pledge, not wholly or in full measure, but very substantially. At the stroke of the midnight hour, when the world sleeps, India will awake to life and freedom. A moment comes, which comes but rarely 5 in history, when we step out from the old to the new, when an age ends, and when the soul of a nation, long suppressed,

solemn very serious and ceremonial

finds utterance. It is fitting that, at this solemn moment, we take the pledge of dedication to the service of India and her people and to the still larger cause of humanity. 10

quest a long, difficult search for sth
striving continually trying very hard to achieve sth

At the dawn of history, India started on her unending quest, and trackless centuries are filled with her striving and the grandeur of her success and her failures. Through good and ill fortune alike, she has never lost sight of that quest or forgotten the ideals which gave her strength. We end today a 15 period of ill fortune and India discovers herself again. The achievement we celebrate today is but a step, an opening of opportunity to the greater triumphs and achievements that await us. Are we brave enough and wise enough to grasp this opportunity and accept the challenge of the future? 20

Freedom and power bring responsibility. The responsibility rests upon this Assembly, a sovereign body representing the sovereign people of India. Before the birth of freedom, we

to endure the pains of labour to suffer the pain of childbirth

have endured all the pains of labour and our hearts are heavy with the memory of this sorrow. Some of those pains con- 25 tinue even now. Nevertheless, the past is over and it is the future that beckons to us now.

incessant never stopping

The future is not one of ease or resting but of incessant striving so that we may fulfil the pledges we have so often taken and the one we shall take today. The service of India means 30 the service of the millions who suffer. It means the ending of poverty and ignorance and disease and inequality of opportu-

the greatest man i.e. Gandhi

nity. The ambition of the greatest man of our generation has been to wipe every tear from every eye. That may be beyond us, but as long as there are tears and suffering, so long our 35 work will not be over.

And so we have to labour and to work, and work hard, to give reality to our dreams. Those dreams are for India, but they are also for the world, for all the nations and peoples are too closely knit together today for any one of them to imagine that it
5 can live apart. Peace has been said to be indivisible; so is freedom, so is prosperity now, and so also is disaster in this one world that can no longer be split into isolated fragments.

To the people of India, whose representatives we are, we make an appeal to join us with faith and confidence in this great
10 adventure. This is no time for petty destructive criticism, no time for ill-will or blaming others. We have to build the noble mansion of free India where all her children may dwell.

petty here: narrow in outlook

to dwell (*fml*) to live somewhere

II.

The appointed day has come – the day appointed by destiny – and India stands forth again, after long slumber and strug-
15 gle, awake, vital, free and independent. The past clings on to us still in some measure and we have to do much before we redeem the pledges we have so often taken. Yet the turning-point is past, and history begins anew for us, the history which we shall live and act and others will write about. It is a
20 fateful moment for us in India, for all Asia and for the world. A new star rises, the star of freedom in the East, a new hope comes into being, a vision long cherished materializes. May the star never set and that hope never be betrayed!

We rejoice in that freedom, even though clouds surround us,
25 and many of our people are sorrow-stricken and difficult problems encompass us. But freedom brings responsibilities and burdens and we have to face them in the spirit of a free and disciplined people.

On this day our first thoughts go to the architect of this free-
30 dom, the Father of our Nation, who, embodying the old spirit of India, held aloft the torch of freedom and lighted up the darkness that surrounded us. We have often been unworthy followers of his and have strayed from his message, but not only we but succeeding generations will remember this mes-
35 sage and bear the imprint in their hearts of this great son of India, magnificent in his faith and strength and courage and humility. We shall never allow that torch of freedom to be blown out, however high the wind or stormy the tempest.

Our next thoughts must be of the unknown volunteers and
40 soldiers of freedom who, without praise or reward, have served India even unto death.

We think also of our brothers and sisters who have been cut off from us by political boundaries and who unhappily can-

slumber sleep

the Father of our Nation i. e. Gandhi
aloft high in the air

humility the quality of not being overly proud or arrogant

not share at present in the freedom that has come. They are of us and will remain of us whatever may happen, and we shall be sharers in their good or ill fortune alike.

The future beckons to us. Whither do we go and what shall be our endeavour? To bring freedom and opportunity to the ⁵ common man, to the peasants and workers of India; to fight and end poverty and ignorance and disease; to build up a prosperous, democratic and progressive nation, and to create social, economic and political institutions which will ensure justice and fullness of life to every man and woman.   10

We have hard work ahead. There is no resting for any one of us till we redeem our pledge in full, till we make all the people of India what destiny intended them to be. We are citizens of a great country on the verge of bold advance, and we have to live up to that high standard. All of us, to whatever religion ¹⁵ we may belong, are equally the children of India with equal rights, privileges and obligations. We cannot encourage communalism or narrow-mindedness, for no nation can be great whose people are narrow in thought or in action.

To the nations and peoples of the world we send greetings ²⁰ and pledge ourselves to cooperate with them in furthering peace, freedom and democracy.

And to India, our much-loved motherland, the ancient, the eternal and the ever-new, we pay our reverent homage and we bind ourselves afresh to her service.   25

to beckon (*fml*) to call
whither (*arch*) to which place

prosperous rich and successful

verge final point beyond which sth is likely to happen
bold brave and confident
advance progress or development

Africa

A. L. Geyer: **A case for apartheid (1953)**

The following speech was given by A. L. Geyer, a supporter of apartheid, at the Rotary Club of London on August 19, 1953. He explains why it is the best policy for all races in South Africa.

As one of the aftermaths of the last war, many people seem to suffer from a neurotic guilt complex with regard to colonies. This has led to a strident denunciation of the Black African's wrongs, real or imaginary, under the white man's rule in Africa. It is a denunciation, so shrill and emotional, that the ⁵

strident forceful and determined
denunciation public statement in which you criticize sb or sth

vast debt owed by Black Africa to those same white men is lost sight of (and, incidentally, the Black African is encouraged to forget that debt). Confining myself to that area of which I know at least a very little, Africa south of the Equator,
5 I shall say this without fear of reasonable contradiction: every millimetre of progress in all that vast area is due entirely to the White Man. You are familiar with the cry that came floating over the ocean from the West – a cry that "colonialism" is outmoded and pernicious, a cry that is being vociferously
10 echoed by a certain gentleman in the East.

May I point out that African colonies are of comparatively recent date? Before that time, Black Africa did have independence for a thousand years and more – and what did she make of it? One problem, I admit, she did solve most effec-
15 tively. There was no overpopulation. Interminable savage intertribal wars, witchcraft, disease, famine, and even cannibalism saw to that.

Let me turn to my subject, to that part of Africa south of the Sahara which, historically, is not part of Black Africa at all –
20 my own country. Its position is unique in Africa as its racial problem is unique in the world.

1. South Africa is no more the original home of its black Africans, the Bantu than it is of its white Africans. Both races went there as colonists and, what is more, as practically con-
25 temporary colonists. In some parts, the Bantu arrived first, in other parts, the Europeans were the first comers.
2. South Africa contains the only independent white nation in all Africa. A nation which has created a highly-developed modern state, and which occupies a position of in-
30 estimable importance.
3. South Africa is the only independent country in the world in which white people are outnumbered by black people. Including all coloured races or peoples, the proportion in Brazil is 20 to 1. In South Africa, it is 1 to 4.

35 This brings me to the question of the future. To me there seem to be two possible lines of development: Apartheid or Partnership. Partnership means Cooperation of the individual citizens within a single community, irrespective of race. [...] [It] demands that there shall be no discrimination what-
40 soever in trade and industry, in the professions and the Public Service. Therefore, whether a man is black or a white African must according to this policy be as irrelevant as whether in London a man is a Scotsman or an Englishman. I take it

pernicious (*fml*) very harmful or evil
a certain gentleman i. e. Jawaharlal Nehru, then Prime Minister of India

interminable continual, never-ending

Bantu general term for over 400 ethnic groups with a common language in Southern Africa

suffrage the right to vote in national elections
loading of the franchise (*fml*) adjusting the value of votes in the elections to give advantages to one group over another
expedient quick and effective way of dealing with a problem

that Partnership must also aim at the eventual disappearance of all social segregation based on race. This policy of Partnership admittedly does not envisage immediate adult suffrage. Obviously, however, the loading of the franchise in order to exclude the great majority of the Bantu could be no worse 5 than a temporary expedient. [...] [In effect] there must one day be black domination, in the sense that power must pass to the immense African majority.

Need I say more to show that this policy of Partnership could, in South Africa, only mean the eventual disappearance of the 10 white South African nation? And will you be greatly surprised if I tell you that this white nation is not prepared to commit national suicide, not even by slow poisoning? The only alternative is a policy of apartheid, the policy of separate develop-

inherent forming a natural part of

ment. The germ of this policy is inherent in almost all of our 15 history, implanted there by the force of circumstances. [...]

self-preservation the desire to stay alive

Apartheid is a policy of self-preservation. We make no apology for possessing that very natural urge. But it is more than that. It is an attempt at self-preservation in a manner that will enable the Bantu to develop fully as a separate people. 20 We believe that, for a long time to come, political power will have to remain with the whites, also in the interest of our still

immature not fully developed

very immature Bantu. But we believe also, in the words of a statement by the Dutch Reformed Church in 1950, a Church that favours apartheid, that "no people in the world worth 25

worth one's salt here: worthy of respect

their salt, would be content indefinitely with no say or only indirect say in the affairs of the State or in the country's socio-economic organisation in which decisions are taken about their interests and their future."

The immediate aim is, therefore, to keep the races outside the 30 Bantu areas apart as far as possible, to continue the process of improving the conditions and standards of living of the Bantu, and to give them greater responsibility for their own local affairs. At the same time, the long-range aim is to develop the Bantu areas both agriculturally and industrially, with the ob- 35 ject of making these areas in every sense the national home

paramount (*fml*) more important than anything else

of the Bantu – areas in which their interests are paramount, in which to an ever greater degree, all professional and other positions are to be occupied by them, and in which they are to receive progressively more and more autonomy. 40

Harold Macmillan: **The wind of change (1960)**

On February 3, 1960, during his tour of Africa in 1960, Harold Macmillan, Britain's then Prime Minister, made this speech in Capetown, attacking the South African policy of apartheid.

It is, as I have said, a special privilege for me to be here in 1960 when you are celebrating what I might call the golden wedding of the Union. At such a time, it is natural and right that you should pause to take stock of your position, to look
5 back at what you have achieved, to look forward to what lies ahead. In the fifty years of their nationhood, the people of South Africa have built a strong economy founded upon a healthy agriculture and thriving and resilient industries.

No one could fall to be impressed with the immense material
10 progress which has been achieved. That all this has been accomplished in so short a time is a striking testimony to the skill, energy and initiative of your people. We in Britain are proud of the contribution we have made to this remarkable achievement. Much of it has been financed by British capi-
15 tal.

[...] As I've travelled around the Union, I have found everywhere, as I expected, a deep preoccupation with what is happening in the rest of the African continent. I understand and sympathise with your interests in these events and your anx-
20 iety about them.

Ever since the break up of the Roman Empire, one of the constant facts of political life in Europe has been the emergence of independent nations. They have come into existence over the centuries in different forms, different kinds of govern-
25 ment, but all have been inspired by a deep, keen feeling of nationalism, which has grown as the nations have grown.

In the twentieth century, and especially since the end of the war, the processes which gave birth to the nation states of Europe have been repeated all over the world. We have seen
30 the awakening of national consciousness in peoples who have for centuries lived in dependence upon some other power. Fifteen years ago, this movement spread through Asia. Many countries there, of different races and civilisations, pressed their claim to an independent national life.

35 Today the same thing is happening in Africa, and the most striking of all the impressions I have formed since I left London a month ago is of the strength of this African national consciousness. In different places, it takes different forms,

The **Union of South Africa** was founded in 1910, so 1960 represented the "golden wedding", i.e. fifty years.

thriving very successful
resilient able to return to strength after difficult times

preoccupation concern

anxiety worry

but it is happening everywhere. The wind of change is blow-
ing through this continent, and whether we like it or not,
this growth of national consciousness is a political fact. We
must all accept it as a fact, and our national policies must

to take account of to
consider particular facts when
making a decision

take account of it. 5

Of course, you understand this better than anyone, you are
sprung from Europe, the home of nationalism, and here in
Africa, you have yourselves created a new nation. Indeed, in
the history of our times, yours will be recorded as the first of
the African nationalists. This tide of national consciousness 10
which is now rising in Africa is a fact, for which both you and
we, and the other nations of the western world are ultimately
responsible.

For its causes are to be found in the achievements of western
civilisation, in the pushing forwards of the frontiers of knowl- 15
edge, the applying of science to the service of human needs,
in the expanding of food production, in the speeding and
multiplying of the means of communication, and perhaps
above all and more than anything else in the spread of education. 20

As I have said, the growth of national consciousness in Africa
is a political fact, and we must accept it as such. That means,
I would judge, that we've got to come to terms with it. I sin-

to come to terms with sth
to accept sth difficult
to imperil to endanger
precarious shaky, unstable

cerely believe that if we cannot do so we may imperil the
precarious balance between the East and West on which the 25
peace of the world depends.

The world today is divided into three main groups. First there
are what we call the Western Powers. You in South Africa and
we in Britain belong to this group, together with our friends
and allies in other parts of the Commonwealth. In the Unit- 30
ed States of America and in Europe, we call it the Free World.
Secondly, there are the Communists – Russia and her satel-
lites in Europe and China whose population will rise by the
end of the next ten years to the staggering total of 800 million. Thirdly, there are those parts of the world whose people 35
are at present uncommitted either to Communism or to our
Western ideas. In this context, we think first of Asia and then
of Africa. As I see it, the great issue in this second half of the
twentieth century is whether the uncommitted peoples of
Asia and Africa will swing to the East or to the West. Will they 40
be drawn into the Communist camp? Or will the great ex-
periments in self-government that are now being made in
Asia and Africa, especially within the Commonwealth, prove

compelling here: irresistible or
forceful

so successful, and by their example so compelling, that the
balance will come down in favour of freedom and order and 45

justice? The struggle is joined, and it is a struggle for the minds of men. What is now on trial is much more than our military strength or our diplomatic and administrative skill. It is our way of life. The uncommitted nations want to see
5 before they choose [...].
I have thought you would wish me to state plainly and with full candour the policy for which we in Britain stand. It may well be that, in trying to do our duty as we see it, we shall sometimes make difficulties for you. If this proves to be so,
10 we shall regret it. But I know that, even so, you would not ask us to flinch from doing our duty.
As a fellow member of the Commonwealth, it is our earnest desire to give South Africa our support and encouragement, but I hope you won't mind my saying frankly that there are
15 some aspects of your policies which make it impossible for us to do this without being false to our own deep convictions about the political destinies of free men to which, in our own territories, we are trying to give effect. I think we ought to, as friends, face together, without seeking to apportion credit or
20 blame, the fact that, in the world of today, this difference of outlook lies between us. [...]

candour honesty

to flinch to draw back from sth unpleasant

Hendrik Verwoerd: **Response to Harold Macmillan's speech (1960)**

In response to Macmillan's speech that criticized South Africa's policy of apartheid, Verwoerd delivered the following speech to the parliament of South Africa.

The tendency in Africa for nations to become independent, and at the same time to do justice to all, does not only mean being just to the black man of Africa, but also to be just to the white man of Africa.
5 We call ourselves European, but actually we represent the white men of Africa. They are the people, not only in the Union but through major portions of Africa, who brought civilisation here, who made the present developments of black nationalists possible. By bringing them education, by
10 showing them this way of life, by bringing in industrial development, by bringing in the ideals which western civilisation has developed itself.

When the white man came to Africa, perhaps to trade, in some cases, perhaps to bring the gospel, he has remained to stay. And particularly we in this southern most portion of Africa, have such a stake here that this is our only motherland, we have nowhere else to go. We set up a country bare, and the Bantu 5 came in this country and settled certain portions for themselves, and it is in line with the thinking of Africa, to grant those fullest rights which we also with you admit all people should have and believe in providing those rights for those people in the fullest degree in that part of southern Africa 10 which their forefathers found for themselves and settled in. But similarly, we believe in balance, we believe in allowing exactly those same full opportunities to remain within the grasp of the white man, who has made all this possible.

Reactions in Britain

Enoch Powell: River of blood (1968)

Powell was a right-wing nationalist who believed that the British Nationality Act had enabled too many immigrants to enter Great Britain. He held this speech on April 20, 1968 in Birmingham and caused enormous public uproar.

constituent a voter in a district represented by an elected official

[...] A week or two ago, I fell into conversation with a constituent, a middle-aged, quite ordinary working man employed in one of our nationalized industries. After a sentence or two about the weather, he suddenly said: "If I had the money to go, I wouldn't stay in this country." 5

deprecator intended to make sb feel less annoyed or disapproving

I made some deprecatory reply, to the effect that even this Government wouldn't last for ever; but he took no notice, and continued: "I have three children, all of them have been through grammar school and two of them married now, with family. I shan't be satisfied till I have seen them settled over- 10 seas. In this country in fifteen or twenty years' time, the black

whip hand control

man will have the whip hand over the white man."

execration abhorrence: hate coupled with disgust

I can already hear the chorus of execration. How dare I say such a horrible thing? How dare I stir up trouble and inflame feelings by repeating such a conversation? 15

The answer is that I do not have the right not to do so. Here is a decent, ordinary fellow Englishman, who in broad daylight in my own town says to me, his Member of Parliament, that this country will not be worth living in for his children.
5 I simply do not have the right to shrug my shoulders and think about something else.

What he is saying, thousands and hundreds of thousands are saying and thinking – not throughout Great Britain, perhaps, but in the areas that are already undergoing the total trans-
10 formation to which there is no parallel in a thousand years of English history.

In fifteen or twenty years, on present trends, there will be in this country 3 ½ million Commonwealth immigrants and their descendants. That is not my figure. That is the official
15 figure given to Parliament by the spokesman of the Registrar General's office. There is no comparable official figure for the year 2000, but it must be in the region of 5 – 7 million, approximately one-tenth of the whole population, and approaching that of Greater London.

20 Of course, it will not be evenly distributed from Margate to Aberystwyth and from Penzance to Aberdeen. Whole areas, towns and parts of towns across England will be occupied by different sections of the immigrant and immigrant-descended population.

25 As time goes on, the proportion of this total who are immigrant descendants, those born in England, who arrived here by exactly the same route as the rest of us, will rapidly increase. Already by 1985, the native-born would constitute the majority. It is this fact above all which creates the ex-
30 treme urgency of action now, of just that kind of action which is hardest for politicians to take, action where the difficulties lie in the present but the evils to be prevented or minimized lie several parliaments ahead.

The natural and rational first question which a nation con-
35 fronted by such a prospect is to ask: "How can its dimensions be reduced?" Granted it be not wholly preventable, can it be limited, bearing in mind that numbers are of the essence: the significance and consequences of an alien element introduced into a country or population are profoundly different accord-
40 ing to whether that element is 1 per cent or 10 per cent.

The answers to the simple and rational question are equally simple and rational: by stopping or virtually stopping, further inflow, and by promoting the maximum outflow. Both answers are part of the official policy of the Conservative
45 Party.

descendant sb who is related to a person who lived a long time ago
Registrar General's Office authority in charge of recording births, deaths and marriages, etc.

Margate, Aberystwyth, Penzance, Aberdeen cities in the south, west, southwest and north of the UK

granted given that

Wolverhampton a city and
metropolitan borough in the
English West Midlands
hence here: in the future

to heap to put a lot of things
on top of each other in an
untidy way
funeral pyre wood heaped
together for burning a dead
body
spouse a husband or wife
to tail off to become gradually
less or fewer and often
disappear completely
voucher here: an official
document issued by UK
immigration allowing the holder
to obtain a visa
per annum ad infinitum
(*latin*) per year forever and ever
fraudulent intended to deceive
people in an illegal way for
personal gain
negligible a very small amount

to tackle to try to deal with a
difficult problem

It almost passes belief that at this moment twenty or thirty
additional immigrant children are arriving from overseas in
Wolverhampton alone every week – and that means fifteen
or twenty additional families of a decade or two hence. Those
whom the gods wish to destroy, they first make mad. We 5
must be mad, literally mad, as a nation to be permitting the
annual inflow of some 50,000 dependants, who are, for the
most part, the material of the future growth of the immigrant-descended population.

It is like watching a nation busily engaged in heaping up its 10
own funeral pyre.

So insane are we that we actually permit unmarried persons
to immigrate for the purpose of founding a family with
spouses and fiancées whom they have never seen. Let no one
suppose that the flow of dependants will automatically tail 15
off. On the contrary, even at the present admission rate of
only 5,000 a year by voucher, there is sufficient for a further
325,000 dependants per annum ad infinitum, without taking
into account the huge reservoir of existing relations in this
country – and I am making no allowance at all for fraudulent 20
entry.

In these circumstances, nothing will suffice but that the total
inflow for settlement should be reduced at once to negligible
proportions, and that the necessary legislative and administrative measures be taken without delay. I stress the words 25
"for settlement". This has nothing to do with the entry of
Commonwealth citizens, any more than of aliens, into this
country, for the purposes of study or of improving their qual-
ifications, like (for instance) the Commonwealth doctors
who, to the advantage of their own countries, have enabled 30
our hospital service to be expanded faster than would otherwise have been possible. These are not, and never have been,
immigrants.

I turn to re-emigration. If all immigration ended tomorrow,
the rate of growth of the immigrant and immigrant-descend- 35
ed population would be substantially reduced, but the pro-
spective size of this element in the population would still
leave the basic character of the national danger unaffected.
This can only be tackled while a considerable proportion of
the total still comprises persons who entered this country 40
during the last ten years or so. Hence the urgency of imple-
menting now the second element of the Conservative Party's
policy: the encouragement of re-emigration.

Nobody can make an estimate of the numbers which, with
generous grants and assistance, would choose either to re- 45

turn to their countries of origin or to go to other countries anxious to receive the manpower and the skills they represent. Nobody knows, because no such policy has yet been attempted. I can only say that, even at present, immigrants
5 in my own constituency from time to time come to me, asking if I can find them assistance to return home. If such a policy were adopted and pursued with the determination which the gravity of the alternative justifies, the resultant outflow could appreciably alter the prospects for the future.
10 It can be no part of any policy that existing families should be kept divided; but there are two directions in which families can be reunited, and if our former and present immigration laws have brought about the division of families, albeit voluntary or semi-voluntarily, we ought to be prepared to ar-
15 range for them to be reunited in their countries of origin.

In short, suspension of immigration and encouragement of re-emigration hang together, logically and humanly, as two aspects of the same approach.

The third element of the Conservative Party's policy is that
20 all who are in this country as citizens should be equal before the law and that there shall be no discrimination or difference made between them by public authority. As Mr. Heath has put it, we will have no "first-class citizens" and "second-class citizens".
25 This does not mean that the immigrant and his descendants should be elevated into a privileged or special class or that the citizen should be denied his right to discriminate in the management of his own affairs between one fellow citizen and another or that he should be subjected to inquisition as
30 to his reasons and motives for behaving in one lawful manner rather than another.

There could be no grosser misconception of the realities than is entertained by those who vociferously demand legislation as they call it "against discrimination", whether they be lead-
35 er-writers of the same kidney and sometimes on the same newspapers which year after year in the 1930s tried to blind this country to the rising peril which confronted it, or archbishops who live in palaces, faring delicately with the bedclothes pulled right over their heads. They have got it exactly
40 and diametrically wrong. The discrimination and the deprivation, the sense of alarm and resentment, lies not with the immigrant population but with those among whom they have come and are still coming.

This is why to enact legislation of the kind before Parliament
45 at this moment is to risk throwing a match on to the gun-

to pursue to continue doing an activity or trying to achieve sth over a long period of time

albeit even though

suspension of officially stopping sth for a period of time

Edward Heath
(1916–2005) Prime Minister of the United Kingdom from 1970–1974

vociferous expressing one's opinions loudly and strongly

kidney here: temperament, kind

peril danger

to fare here: to perform a task

diametric here: at the opposite end

franchise (*fml*) the legal right to vote

by hook or by crook whatever it takes

by default happening automatically if nothing is done to change it

to redress a grievance to set right an earlier wrongdoing
disgruntled annoyed or disappointed
agent provocateur here: troublemaker
to pillory to publicly criticize, esp. in newspapers

powder. The kindest thing that can be said about those who propose and support it is they know not what they do.

Nothing is more misleading than comparison between the Commonwealth immigrant in Britain and the American Negro. The Negro population of the United States, which was 5 already in existence before the United States became a nation, started literally as slaves and were later given the franchise and other rights of citizenship, to the exercise of which they have only gradually and still incompletely come. The Commonwealth immigrant came to Britain as a full citizen, 10 to a country which knows no discrimination between one citizen and another, and he entered instantly into the possession of the rights of every citizen, from the vote to free treatment under the National Health Service. Whatever drawbacks attended the immigrants – and they were drawbacks 15 which did not, and do not, make admission into Britain by hook or by crook appear less than desirable – arose not from the law or from public policy or from administration but from those personal circumstances and accidents which cause, and always will cause, the fortunes and experience of 20 one man to be different for another's.

But while to the immigrant, entry to this country was admission to privileges and opportunities eagerly sought, the impact upon the existing population was very different. For reasons which they could not comprehend, and in pursu- 25 ance of a decision by default, on which they were never consulted, they found themselves made strangers in their own country. They found their wives unable to obtain hospital beds in childbirth, their children unable to obtain school places, their homes and neighbourhoods changed beyond 30 recognition, their plans and prospects for the future defeated; at work they found that employers hesitated to apply to the immigrant worker the standards of discipline and competence required of the native-born worker; they began to hear, as time went by, more and more voices which told them that 35 they were now the unwanted.

On top of this, they now learn that a one-way privilege is to be established by Act of Parliament: a law, which cannot, and is not intended, to operate to protect them or redress their grievances, is to be enacted to give the stranger, the disgrun- 40 tled and the agent provocateur the power to pillory them for their private actions.

In the hundreds upon hundreds of letters I received when I last spoke on this subject two or three months ago, there was one striking feature which was largely new and which I find 45

ominous. All Members of Parliament are used to the typical anonymous correspondent; but what surprised and alarmed me was the high proportion of ordinary, decent, sensible people, writing a rational and often well-educated letter, who
5 believed that they had to omit their address because it was dangerous to have committed themselves to paper to a Member of Parliament agreeing with the views I had expressed, and that they would risk either penalties or reprisals if they were known to have done so.
10 The sense of being a persecuted minority, which is growing among ordinary English people in the areas of the country which are affected, is something that those without direct experience can hardly imagine. [...]

To be integrated into a population means to become for all
15 practical purposes indistinguishable from its other members. Now, at all times, where there are marked physical differences, especially of colour, integration is difficult though, over a period, not impossible. There are among the Commonwealth immigrants who have come to live here in the
20 last fifteen years or so, many thousands whose wish and purpose is to be integrated and whose every thought and endeavour is bent in that direction. But to imagine that such a thing enters the heads of a great and growing majority of immigrants and their descendants is a ludicrous misconception,
25 and a dangerous one to boot. [...]

As I look ahead, I am filled with foreboding. Like the Roman, I seem to see "the River Tiber foaming with much blood". That tragic and intractable phenomenon which we watch with horror on the other side of the Atlantic but which there
30 is interwoven with the history and existence of the States itself, is coming upon us here by our own volition and our own neglect.

Indeed, it has all but come. In numerical terms, it will be of American proportions long before the end of the century.
35 Only resolute and urgent action will avert it even now.

Whether there will be the public will to demand and obtain that action, I do not know.

All I know is that to see, and not to speak, would be the great betrayal.

---

ominous threatening

to omit leave out

reprisal sth violent or harmful done to punish sb for sth bad they have done to you, revenge

indistinguishable not able to be seen as different

ludicrous completely unreasonable, stupid, or wrong
to boot in addition to everything else mentioned

"the River Tiber" Virgil's Aeneid, bk. 6, l. 86: "Et Thybrim multo spumantem sanguine cerno." The phrase "rivers of blood" was also used by, among others, Thomas Jefferson and Winston Churchill.

intractable difficult to control or manage
volition desire, willingness
to avert to stop sth bad happening

Tony Blair: Immigration and politics do not make easy bedfellows (2004)

On April 27, 2004, the then Prime Minister Tony Blair held this speech at the Confederation of British industry. He speaks about the issue of immigration.

Immigration and politics do not make easy bedfellows. They never have. We need few reminders of what can happen when the politics of immigration gets out of hand.

Let us also be very clear. Those who warned of disaster back in the 1960s and 1970s if migration was not stopped, who 5 said Britain would never accept a multi-racial society, have been proved comprehensively wrong.

On the other hand, there is no doubt that on the doorstep, in local communities, immigration has suddenly become very high on the agenda. Why? 10

It is not, incidentally, an exclusively British issue.

This is a worldwide phenomenon. [...]

And beneath the surface, we all know as politicians, certainly on the centre left, what we fear: that concern slips into prejudice, and becomes racism. But we cannot simply dismiss any 15 concern about immigration as racism.

In part, what has put immigration back on the agenda – with public concern at its highest since the 1970s – is that there are real, not imagined abuses of the system that lead to a sense of genuine unfairness. 20

There were real problems with asylum; some immigration procedures have clearly been at fault; some rules, introduced for entirely legitimate reasons, have been subject to systematic and often criminal fraud. Many of these systems simply need bringing up to date. 25

Then there are high profile examples of the absurd – not many in number but very damaging in terms of impact – like radical clerics coming here to preach religious hate; people staying here to peddle support for terrorism.

The combination of all these things – with the reporting of 30 them not exactly calculated to douse the flames of concern – lead to a crunch point. That is where we are now.

The vast bulk of the British people are not racist. It is in their nature to be moderate. But they expect Government to respond to their worries. They can accept migration that is 35 controlled and selective. They accept and welcome migrants who play by the rules. But they will not accept abuse or absurdity and why should they?

So now is the time to make the argument for controlled migration simultaneous with tackling the abuses we can identify; and then, longer term, put in place a system that gives us the best guarantee of future integrity in our migration policy.

That is why we have begun a top to bottom analysis of the immigration system, how it operates, how it can be improved, how it can agree with migration where it is in our country's interests and prevent it where it isn't. One thing already is clear: the overwhelming majority migrate in and often out of Britain fairly and in accordance with the rules. But there are areas of abuse and we can and should deal with them.

We are putting in place a strategy – globally, nationally and locally – to ensure migration works for Britain today and in the future.

We will neither be Fortress Britain, nor will we be an open house. Where necessary, we will tighten the immigration system. Where there are abuses we will deal with them, so that public support for the controlled migration that benefits Britain is maintained.

Our strategy has a number of interlocking elements:

A recognition of the benefits that controlled migration brings not just to the economy but to delivering the public and private services on which we rely.

Being clear that all those who come here to work and study must be able to support themselves. There can be no access to state support or housing for the economically inactive.

We will continue to tackle abuses in the asylum system, including through the legislation currently before Parliament which will establish a single tier of appeal and clamp down on asylum seekers who deliberately destroy their documents and lie about their identity.

Action on illegal immigration through the introduction of ID cards and millions invested in strengthening our border controls in ports and airports across the world: and heightened enforcement in the UK too.

Celebrating the major achievements of migrants in this country and the success of our uniquely British model of diversity. But alongside that, an explicit expectation that rights must be balanced by responsibilities. That there are clear obligations that go alongside British residency and ultimately citizenship – to reject extremism and intolerance and make a positive contribution to UK society.

An acknowledgement that there is no longer a neat separa-

to maintain to make sure sth continues in the same way or at the same standard as before

to clamp down on to become tough with, make the rules stricter

tion between the domestic and the international. In a world of global interdependence our policies on migration cannot be isolated from our policies on international development or EU enlargement.

But I want to start today with some facts – for too often the 5 debate about immigration is characterised by a vacuum of reliable information which can all too easily be filled by myth. To give just one example a recent MORI poll found that people estimated the proportion of ethnic minorities in Britain as 23 % when the real figure is a third of that at 8 %. 10 So fact one; the movement of people and labour into and out of the UK is, and always has been, absolutely essential to our economy.

Visitors from outside the European Union spent £6.8bn in the UK in 2002 and those from within the European Union 15 billions more. Overseas students spend over £3bn on fees and goods and services a year on top of that.

Indeed according to the Treasury, our economic growth rate would be almost 0.5 % lower for the next two years if migration ceased. Lower growth means less individual and family 20 prosperity, and less revenue to spend on public services.

And the economic contribution of visitors and migrants is nothing new. At crucial points over the past century and beyond we have relied on migrants to supply essential capital to our economy and plug the labour gaps when no others 25 could be found.

When the Bank of England was founded, for example, in 1694, 10 per cent of its initial capital was put up by 123 French Huguenot merchants who had already transformed Britain's textile and paper industries. 30

In the mid 19th century, more than 900,000 Irish immigrants settled in England – and became a mainstay of our armed forces – 30 % by 1830.

157,000 Poles came to Britain immediately after the Second World War, soon followed by the Italians – all filling essential 35 gaps in a labour market – in our mines and steel mills and brick works.

And they were followed in the 1950s and 1960s by workers from the West Indies and South Asia who found jobs in electrical engineering, food and drink plants, car manufacturing, 40 paper and rubber mills and plastic works, fuelling the postwar economic boom that backed up MacMillan's claim that "we'd never had it so good".

And then since the late eighties and nineties it is I.T. and finance professionals from the U.S., India, the EU and else- 45

MORI the second largest opinion poll research company in the UK

Treasury the government department responsible for collecting, managing and spending public revenues

revenue income

to plug to fill

Harold MacMillan (1894–1986) British Prime Minister from 1957–1963 (cf. p. 99)

where who have driven London's growth as the financial centre of the world in a highly competitive global market for financial services.

5 As CBI Director Digby Jones says in today's FT "using control-led migration to help reduce skill gaps and stimulate economic growth in geographical areas that might otherwise have problems is nothing more than common sense".

And never forget those migrants from the Commonwealth and Eastern Europe who gave more than just their labour.

10 138,000 Indian soldiers served the British Army on the Western Front in the First World War. Thousands of Polish airmen flew alongside the RAF during World War II. And it was Polish mathematicians who helped break the enigma code.

So each decade brings its own particular needs, its own skills 15 gap and our immigration system too must keep responding to these gaps in a targeted and controlled way.

Which brings me to my second fact. This country is already highly selective about who is allowed in to the UK to work, study or settle. Almost 220,000 people were refused entry 20 clearance by our posts abroad in 2002 – more than treble the number in 1992. Thousands more were turned back at airports by airlines working with IND's network of liaison officers.

Those wishing to work or study in the UK or to marry a UK national must show that they are able to support themselves 25 without access to state funds. And they must satisfy our overseas embassies that they will leave the UK at the end of their stay.

Employers wishing to employ a worker from outside the EU must demonstrate that they have advertised that position in 30 the UK and failed to attract a suitably qualified British applicant before they are given a work permit.

The number of low-skilled workers that are allowed into the country from outside the EU remains small compared to other countries and is controlled by strict quotas – all of 35 which we will now cut significantly following the expansion of the EU.

My third fact is that, in international terms, the UK is not a particularly high migration country. Even today. We have lower levels of foreign-born nationals as a proportion of our 40 total population than France, Germany or the US.

And the same applies to our work force. Only 8 % of our work force is foreign born compared to 15 % in the US and almost 25 % in Australia.

Indeed, trends in net migration to the UK over the past two 45 or three years have been in line with those of our European

CBI Confederation of British Industry, similar to the German *Handelskammer*

FT Financial Times

treble three times the amount

IND Immigration and Nationality Directorate

neighbours like Germany, Sweden and the Netherlands and significantly less than for Spain, Ireland, Australia or the US – where migration increased by 50% in the 1990s.

So those who say migration is out of control or that the UK is taking more people than other countries are simply wrong. 5 As are those who suggest that we exert no control over who comes here.

Those who do come here make a huge contribution, particularly to our public services. So, fact four: far from always or even mainly being a burden on our health or education sys- 10 tems – migrant workers are often the very people delivering those services.

Take the nursing staff from the West Indies recruited by then health minister, Enoch Powell in the 1960s. By 1968, there were almost 19,000 trainee nurses and midwives born over- 15 seas – 35% of whom were from the West Indies and 15% from Ireland. Now, a quarter of all health professionals are overseas born.

Or consider the 11,000 overseas teachers now working in schools in England. Or the 23% of staff in our HE institutions 20 who are non-UK nationals – that's 33,530 out of 143,150.

Our public services would be close to collapse without their contribution.

And there is an important fifth fact. Migration is not all one way. Britain is a nation of outward migration as well as in- 25 ward migration. Over the past two centuries, millions of Britons have left the UK to seek work in America, Canada, Australia and further afield.

There are for example 200,000 UK passport holders living in New Zealand alone and UK applicants account for almost a 30 quarter of employment visas issued each year by the New Zealand government. The UK remains the largest source country for skilled migrants to Australia.

UK nationals form the third most important group of immigrant workers to Canada – behind only the USA and Mexico 35 in 2002 and hundreds of thousands of people from the UK live and work in mainland Europe.

Many of these workers will return to the UK. Others will stay on and marry local residents. Between them they will send back millions of pounds in remittances – contributing not 40 just to the economic prosperity of their host country – but to the UK too.

So these are the facts. Population mobility and migration has been crucial to our economic success, migration levels in the UK are in line with comparable countries, we are already se- 45

midwife (pl wives) a person trained to help women in childbirth

HE institution Higher Education institution, e.g. university, technical college, etc.

remittance money sent to sb living in another place, usually the immigrant's family in the homeland

lective about who comes into Britain and many that do are essential to our public services. But precisely because stopping migration altogether would be disastrous for our country and economy, it is all the more vital to ensure the system
5 is not abused. There are real concerns; they are not figments of racist imagination; and they have to be tackled precisely in order to sustain a balanced and sensible argument about migration.

figment *Hirngespinst*

Biographies

Mahatma Gandhi (1869–1948) is often referred to as the father of India. He was the pioneer of resistance through means of civil disobedience. Gandhi studied for a brief period of time at University College London. After an unsuccessful time as a lawyer in Bombay, he went to South Africa (1893–1914), where he first employed his ideas of peaceful civil disobedience in the Indians' struggle for civil rights. After returning to India, Gandhi eventually became the leader of the Indian National Congress, fighting for many social causes and above all for India's independence from foreign domination. On January 30th, 1948 he was assassinated in New Delhi.

Clement Richard Attlee, 1st Earl Attlee (1883–1967) was Prime Minister of the UK from 1945 to 1951. He was also the first Labour Prime Minister to serve a full Parliamentary term. Among his most significant projects, he undertook the nationalisation of several industries and public institutions. His government also created the National Health Service.

Winston Churchill (1874–1965) was one of the most important leaders in modern British and world history. He was elected as a Member of Parliament in 1900 for the Conservative Party; however, in 1904, he became a member of the Liberal Party. In 1925, he changed parties again and rejoined the Conservatives. When he helped break the Great Strike in 1926, he became the enemy of many trade union members and workers. In 1940, he was elected Prime Minister and led Britain through World War II. In 1945, he lost the election because it seemed that many Britons did not believe he would be able to lead them in the after-war times. However, in 1951, he was re-elected as Prime Minister, serving until 1955. He was not only an outstanding politician but also a brilliant historian and writer. During his second term in office, he even won the Nobel Prize in Literature (1953) for his many books on history.

Jawaharlal Nehru (1889–1964) was a barrister educated in England. In the early 1920s, he met Gandhi and became his follower and friend, and later, was one of the most important leaders of the Indian Independence Movement. In 1947 he became the First Prime Minister of India when India won its independence in 1947, staying in office until he died. Two years after his death, his daughter Indira Gandhi also became India's Prime Minister.

Harold Macmillan (1894–1986) was from a humble background. He joined the Conservative Party and was first Minister for Housing, then Minister of Defence and Foreign Secretary before he became Prime Minister in 1957, after his predecessor Anthony Eden had resigned. In 1963, he himself resigned due to health problems.

Hendrik Verwoerd (1901–1966) emigrated to South Africa from the Netherlands when he was two years old. He was Prime Minister of South Africa from 1958–1966 and is regarded as the architect of modern apartheid. While he was Prime Minister, the ANC was banned and Nelson Mandela was tried for treason and sent to prison. In 1966, he was stabbed to death in the House of Assembly by a clerk.

Enoch Powell (1912–1998) was a right-wing British politician and Conservative Party Member of Parliament between 1950 and 1974, before becoming an Ulster Unionist MP from 1974–1987. A Day after his *River of Blood* speech, the then Prime Minister, Sir Edward Heath, sacked him from his Shadow Cabinet and Powell never again held a senior political post.

Tony Blair (*1953): At just 30 years of age, Tony Blair won a seat in the 1983 General Election. In 1997, he led the Labour Party to a landslide victory in the General Election after 18 years in Opposition. This meant that, at the age of 43 Tony Blair became one of the youngest Prime Ministers in the history of Great Britain. He stepped back from office in June 2007.

The global threat of terrorism

Rudy Giuliani: New York city was viciously attacked (2001)

Two weeks after the terrorist attacks on the World Trade Center in New York, Mayor Rudy Giuliani delivered the following speech on October 1st, 2001.

vicious violent and cruel in a way that hurts sb physically
unprovoked without reason or previous attack

condolence expression of sympathy with sb suffering grief, esp. after a death

Pearl Harbor important US naval base in Hawaii, which was suddenly attacked by Japanese planes in December 1941. This led the US to start fighting in World War II.

D-Day 6th June, 1944. In World War II, the day the Allies landed in France to begin the spread of their forces throughout Europe.

inclusive including a wide variety of people and thing [≠ exclusive]
jeopardy danger

to prey on to have a bad or harmful influence on

[...] On September 11th 2001, New York City – the most diverse City in the world – was viciously attacked in an unprovoked act of war. More than five thousand innocent men, women, and children of every race, religion, and ethnicity are lost. Among these were people from 80 different nations. 5 To their representatives here today, I offer my condolences to you as well on behalf of all New Yorkers who share this loss with you. This was the deadliest terrorist attack in history. It claimed more lives than Pearl Harbor or D-Day.

This was not just an attack on the City of New York or on the 10 United States of America. It was an attack on the very idea of a free, inclusive, and civil society.

It was a direct assault on the founding principles of the United Nations itself. The Preamble to the U.N. Charter states that this organization exists "to reaffirm faith in fundamen- 15 tal human rights, in the dignity and worth of the human person [...] to practice tolerance and live together in peace as good neighbors [...] [and] to unite our strength to maintain international peace and security."

Indeed, this vicious attack places in jeopardy the whole pur- 20 pose of the United Nations.

Terrorism is based on the persistent and deliberate violation of fundamental human rights. With bullets and bombs – and now with hijacked airplanes – terrorists deny the dignity of human life. Terrorism preys particularly on cultures and com- 25 munities that practice openness and tolerance. Their targeting of innocent civilians mocks the efforts of those who seek to live together in peace as neighbors. It defies the very notion of being a neighbor.

This massive attack was intended to break our spirit. It has
5 not done that. It has made us stronger, more determined and more resolved.

The bravery of our firefighters, our police officers, our emergency workers, and civilians we may never learn of, in saving over 25,000 lives that day – carrying out the most effective
10 rescue operation in our history – inspires all of us. I am very honored to have with me, as their representative, the Fire Commissioner of New York City, Tom Von Essen, and the Police Commissioner of New York City, Bernard Kerik.

The determination, resolve, and leadership of President
15 George W. Bush has unified America and all decent men and women around the world.

The response of many of your nations – your leaders and people – spontaneously demonstrating in the days after the attack your support for New York and America, and your un-
20 derstanding of what needs to be done to remove the threat of terrorism, gives us great, great hope that we will prevail.

The strength of America's response, please understand, flows from the principles upon which we stand.

Americans are not a single ethnic group.
25 Americans are not of one race or one religion.

Americans emerge from all your nations.

We are defined as Americans by our beliefs – not by our ethnic origins, our race or our religion. Our beliefs in religious freedom, political freedom, and economic freedom – that's
30 what makes an American. Our belief in democracy, the rule of law, and respect for human life – that's how you become an American. It is these very principles – and the opportunities these principles give to so many to create a better life for themselves and their families – that make America, and New
35 York, a "shining city on a hill."

There is no nation, and no City, in the history of the world that has seen more immigrants, in less time, than America. People continue to come here in large numbers to seek freedom, opportunity, decency, and civility.
40 Each of your nations – I am certain – has contributed citizens to the United States and to New York. I believe I can take every one of you someplace in New York City, where you can find someone from your country, someone from your village or town, that speaks your language and practises your reli-
45 gion. In each of your lands there are many who are Ameri-

to mock to ridicule, make fun of

commissioner sb who is officially in charge of a government department

George W. Bush (*1946) the 43rd President of the US (since 2000) (cf. pp. 125f.)

to prevail to be successful in the end, esp. a person, idea or principle

"shining city on a hill" reference to a famous phrase from John Winthrop's sermon "A Model of Christian Charity" that he read in 1630 to about 700 people who had just reached Massachusetts, where they wanted to establish their Puritan community

decency polite, honest, and respectful moral behaviour and attitudes

commitment a promise to do sth or to behave in a particular way

to gain a foothold to reach a secure position that can lead to further progress

deterrent Abschreckungsmittel

to condone to accept or forgive behaviour that most people think is morally wrong
to ostracize to refuse to deal with

rubble the remains of sth destroyed, esp. a building

World Trade Center a group of buildings in Manhattan, New York City, which included two very tall skyscrapers (The Twin Towers) that were destroyed by terrorists in 2001

cans in spirit, by virtue of their commitment to our shared principles.

It is tragic and perverse that it is because of these very principles – particularly our religious, political and economic freedoms – that we find ourselves under attack by terrorists. 5

Our freedom threatens them, because they know that, if our ideas of freedom gain a foothold among their people, it will destroy their power. So they strike out against us to keep those ideas from reaching their people.

The best long-term deterrent to terrorism – obviously – is the 10 spread of our principles of freedom, democracy, the rule of law, and respect for human life. The more that spreads around the globe, the safer we will all be. These are very powerful ideas and once they gain a foothold, they cannot be stopped.

In fact, the rise that we have seen in terrorism and terrorist 15 groups, I believe, is in no small measure a response to the spread of these ideas of freedom and democracy to many nations, particularly over the past 15 years.

The terrorists have no ideas or ideals with which to combat freedom and democracy. So their only defense is to strike out 20 against innocent civilians, destroying human life in massive numbers and hoping to deter all of us from our pursuit and expansion of freedom.

But the long-term deterrent of spreading our ideals throughout the world is just not enough, and may never be realized, 25 if we do not act – and act together – to remove the clear and present danger posed by terrorism and terrorists.

The United Nations must hold accountable any country that supports or condones terrorism otherwise you will fail in your primary mission as peacekeeper. 30

It must ostracize any nation that supports terrorism.

It must isolate any nation that remains neutral in the fight against terrorism.

Now is the time, in the words of the UN Charter, "to unite our strength to maintain international peace and security." 35

This is not a time for further study or vague directives. The evidence of terrorism's brutality and inhumanity – of its contempt for life and the concept of peace – is lying beneath the rubble of the World Trade Center less than two miles from where we meet today. 40

Look at that destruction, that massive, senseless, cruel loss of human life [...] and then I ask you to look in your hearts and recognize that there is no room for neutrality on the issue of terrorism. You're either with civilization or with terrorists.

On one side is democracy, the rule of law, and respect for human life; on the other is tyranny, arbitrary executions, and mass murder.

We're right and they're wrong. It's as simple as that.

5 And by that I mean that America and its allies are right about democracy, about religious, political, and economic freedom. The terrorists are wrong, and in fact evil, in their mass destruction of human life in the name of addressing alleged injustices.

alleged (*fml*) claimed but not yet proven, esp. crimes or facts

10 Let those who say that we must understand the reasons for terrorism come with me to the thousands of funerals we are having in New York City and explain those insane, maniacal reasons to the children who will grow up without fathers and mothers, to the parents who have had their children ripped

15 from them for no reason at all.

Instead, I ask each of you to allow me to say at those funerals that your nation stands with America in making a solemn promise and pledge that we will achieve unconditional victory over terrorism and terrorists. [...]

pledge (*fml*) promise, esp. one made publicly or officially

20 So from the first day of this attack, an attack on New York and America, and I believe an attack on the basic principles that underlie this organization, I have told the people of New York that we should not allow this to divide us, because then we would really lose what this City is all about. We have very

25 strong and vibrant Arab and Muslim communities in New York City. They are an equally important part of the life of our City. We respect their religious beliefs. We respect everybody's religious beliefs – that's what America's about, that's what New York City is about. I have urged New Yorkers not to

30 engage in any form of group blame or group hatred. This is exactly the evil that we are confronting with these terrorists. And if we are going to prevail over terror, our ideals, principles, and values must transcend all forms of prejudice. This is a very important part of the struggle against terrorism.

to transcend to rise above, be better than

35 This is not a dispute between religions or ethnic groups. All religions, all decent people, are united in their desire to achieve peace, and understand that we have to eliminate terrorism. We're not divided about this. [...]

I say to people across the country and around the world: if

40 you were planning to come to New York sometime in the future, come here now. Come to enjoy our thousands of restaurants, museums, theaters, sporting events, and shopping [...] but also come to take a stand against terrorism.

We need to heed the words of a hymn that I, and the Police

45 Commissioner, and the Fire Commissioner, have heard at the

to heed (*fml*) to pay attention to sb's advice or warning

many funerals and memorial services that we've gone to in the last two weeks. The hymn begins, "Be Not Afraid."

Freedom from Fear is a basic human right. We need to re-assert our right to live free from fear with greater confidence and determination than ever before [...] here in New York 5 City [...] across America [...] and around the World. With one clear voice, unanimously, we need to say that we will not give in to terrorism.

Surrounded by our friends of every faith, we know that this is not a clash of civilizations; it is a conflict between murderers 10 and humanity.

This is not a question of retaliation or revenge. It is a matter of justice leading to peace. The only acceptable result is the complete and total eradication of terrorism.

New Yorkers are strong and resilient. We are unified. And we 15 will not yield to terror. We do not let fear make our decisions for us.

We choose to live in freedom.

Thank you, and God bless you.

> **to reassert** to state a fact or opinion again, often more strongly or more clearly

> **retaliation** action against sb who has done sth bad to you, revenge
> **eradication** getting rid of sth completely such as a disease or a social problem
> **resilient** able to become strong, happy, or successful again after a difficult situation

Osama Bin Laden: Statement to the "infidel" nations (2001)

On October 7, 2001, 26 days after the terrorist attacks on the World Trade Center and the Pentagon, Osama Bin Laden addressed the western world with the following public statement.

> **infidel** an offensive word for sb who has a different religion from you

> **to besiege** to surround an area, esp. a city or castle, with military force until the people inside let you take control

The nations of infidels have all united against Muslims. You American people – can you ask yourselves why [there is] all this hate against America and Israel? The answer is clear and very simple, that America has committed so many crimes against the nations of Muslims. 5

America is the head of criminals by creating Israel – this continuous crime for 50 years. The government which is besieging the people of Iraq and killing them. Why [is] your government [...] supporting the rotten governments of our countries? What happened in the United States is a natural reaction 10 to the ignorant policy of the United States. If it continues with this policy, the sons of Islam will not stop their struggle. The American people have to know that what is happening to them now is the result of their support of this policy.

The war against Afghanistan and Osama Bin Laden is a war on Islam. This is a new battle, a great battle, similar to the great battles of Islam, like the conquest of Jerusalem. I believe that there is only one God and there is no prophet but Mo-
5 hammed. America was hit by God in one of its softest spots. America is full of fear from its north to its south, from its west to its east. Thank God for that. This is something, very little, of what we have tasted for decades. Since nearly 80 years we have been tasting this humility.
10 They [Americans] support the murder against the victims so God has given back to them what they deserve. I say that the matter is very clear. That every Muslim after this and after what the officials in America stated, with the head of the in-fidels, Bush, they come out with their men and equipment
15 and they even encourage countries calling themselves Mus-lims against us. They come out to fight Islam in the name of fighting terrorism. These events have split the whole world into two camps: the camps of belief and the camps of disbe-lief. Every Muslim should support his religion and now the
20 wind of change has blown up to the Arabian peninsula. I say by God the great, America will never dream, not those who live in America will never taste security and safety unless we feel security and safety in our lands and in Palestine.

Mohammed also Muhammad, (?570–632) an Arab holy man, born in Mecca, who started the religion of Islam and is its most important Prophet

George W. Bush (*1946) the 43rd President of the US (since 2000) (cf. pp. 125f.)

Colin L. Powell: The United States is taking on the fight against terrorism (2001)

On November 12, 2001, two months after the terrorist attacks on the World Trade Center in New York, Colin Powell delivered the following speech to the United Nations Security Council.

[...] Mr. President, fellow ministers, friends and allies in the coalition against terrorism, action is needed and action is needed now. Two months ago yesterday, citizens from many of the nations present in this room were victims of savage
5 attacks by terrorists here in New York. All of your delegations saw and felt the results of that violence, the wreckage that still smolders less than two miles from this chamber.
Yesterday, President Bush joined by Secretary General Annan and the President of the General Assembly, Foreign Minister
10 Han, commemorated at the site the loss of over 500 of your citizens and the thousands of other innocents who lost their

The United Nations (UN) an international organization that tries to find peaceful solutions to world problems

On **September 11, 2001**, terrorists used planes to attack New York and Washington.

to smolder to burn slowly with thick smoke but no flame

to commemorate to do sth to show that you remember and respect sb important or an important event in the past

lives on that day. Those who seek to define terrorism need look no further. No one can defend such heartless acts against innocent people. This was not about a clash of civilizations or religions; it was an attack on civilization and religion themselves. This is what terrorism means.   5

And now let me share with you what the United States is doing about it and what we hope others will do. The United States is taking the fight against terrorism directly to the terrorists and to their supporters. We have declared war on all terrorist organizations with a global reach.   10

As President Bush made clear to the General Assembly, because these organizations are global, we need the support of all of our partners in the international community. Specifically, we need the help of police forces, intelligence services and banking systems around the world to isolate and eradi- 15 cate our common enemies wherever they may hide.

The United States is grateful that so many nations and so many international organizations have responded so quickly and so forcefully. The American people were heartened by worldwide solidarity after the attacks. The swift action taken 20 by this body and by the General Assembly on September 12th made clear that the perpetrators and supporters of terrorism will be held accountable.

The Security Council took a critical step forward by its adoption of Resolution 1373 a little over two weeks after the at- 25 tacks. Resolution 1373 is a mandate to change fundamentally how the international community responds to terrorism. It requires us to cooperate to target terrorists' ability to solicit and move funds, to find safe haven, to acquire weapons and to move across international borders.   30

For many, implementation will involve complicated and difficult challenges to their financial and legal systems, changes to the established ways of doing things, changes aimed at choking off the funding and weaponry that sustain these terrorist groups, changes in the way we cooperate to find and 35 bring terrorists to justice and to safeguard borders. The Security Council has already gotten off to an excellent start by setting up a committee under able chairmanship to make the call for concerted action and reality.

States are starting to work together to cut off the financial 40 resources that are the oxygen of terrorist groups. We have already seen council members support the immediate freezing of the assets of over 120 persons and entities that the United States identified to the United Nations Afghan Sanctions Committee. The council is well situated to coordinate 45

to eradicate to completely get rid of sb or sth such as an enemy, disease or a social problem

to hearten to give strength, hope and courage to

perpetrator (*fml*) sb who does sth morally wrong or illegal
accountable responsible for one's actions

implementation the act of putting into effect changes that have been officially decided upon
to choke off here: to cut off the supply of
to sustain to help to survive

asset sth of value that is owned by sb

specialized training and assistance to help countries deal with rapid financial flows and regulatory loopholes.

To be effective, 1373 demands a new resolve. As President Bush said, its obligations are urgent and binding. States must
5 now work together, both bilaterally and multilaterally. But the war on terrorism starts within each of our respective sovereign borders. It will be fought with increased support for democracy programs, judicial reform, conflict resolution, poverty alleviation, economic reform and health and educa-
10 tion programs. All of these together deny the reason for terrorists to exist or to find safe havens within those borders.

The United States stands ready to provide technical assistance ranging from aviation security to financial tracking measures and law enforcement. We welcome initiatives by
15 others in these fields and we are ready at any time to exchange information about terrorism and to cooperate in other ways to combat the common enemy, the common threats that we all face.

There is more. We must consider the integrity of internatio-
20 nal transmission systems such as the mail system. We must consider the essential nature of the Internet when phones and mail fail. A few weeks ago, such subjects might have elicited little attention. Today, we can understand that inaction can have grave consequences.
25 In each of these areas, there are important roles for the United Nations and for each of our countries to play. We are grateful for the help of the many who have joined in the fight. We believe out of this great tragedy, a new common purpose has arisen. No greater threat to international peace and security
30 exists in the world today. And, through this body, we have established and are establishing the tools to build a more robust defense. It is time now to put those tools to work.

Thank you very much, Mr. President.

---

loophole a small mistake in a law that makes it possible to legally avoid doing what the law is supposed to make you do
resolve (*fml*) strong determination to succeed in doing sth

alleviation the act of reducing sth unpleasant

law enforcement the job of making sure that laws are obeyed

integrity (*fml*) here: the reliability and safety

to elicit to succeed in getting information or a reaction from sb, esp. when this is difficult
grave serious

Tony Blair: **My divisive decision to go to war in Iraq (2004)**

Prime minister Tony Blair delivered the following speech on March 14, 2004 in Sedgefield to justify military action in Iraq and to warn of the continued threat of global terrorism

divisive causing a lot of disagreement between people

preoccupation worry

fervent believing or feeling sth very strongly and sincerely
WMD (*pl*) weapons of mass destruction
to warrant to justify or make necessary

UN the United Nations, an international organization that tries to find peaceful solutions to world problems

Saddam Hussein (1937–2007) President of Iraq from 1979 to 2003. Because the US and Britain believed that he was preventing UN weapons inspectors from checking whether Iraq had weapons of mass destruction, they invaded Iraq and took him prisoner. He was put on trial by the Iraqi authorities in 2003, charged with crimes against the Iraqi people and executed in 2007.

to contain here: to prevent sb or sth from causing further damage
abhorrent completely unacceptable because it seems morally wrong

No decision I have ever made in politics has been as divisive as the decision to go to war in Iraq. It remains deeply divisive today, I know a large part of the public want to move on. Rightly they say the Government should concentrate on the issues that elected us in 1997: the economy, jobs, living 5 standards, health, education, crime. I share that view, and we are. But I know too that the nature of this issue over Iraq, stirring such bitter emotions as it does, can't just be swept away as ill-fitting the preoccupations of the man and woman on the street. This is not simply because of the gravity of war; 10 or the continued engagement of British troops and civilians in Iraq; or even because of reflections made on the integrity of the Prime Minister. It is because it was in March 2003 and remains my fervent view that the nature of the global threat we face in Britain and round the world is real and existential 15 and it is the task of leadership to expose it and fight it, whatever the political cost; and that the true danger is not to any single politician's reputation, but to our country if we now ignore this threat or erase it from the agenda in embarrassment at the difficulties it causes. [...] 20

Iraq in March 2003 was an immensely difficult judgement. It was divisive because it was difficult. I have never disrespected those who disagreed with the decision. Sure, some were anti-American; some against all wars. But there was a core of sensible people who, faced with this decision, would 25 have gone the other way, for sensible reasons. Their argument is one I understand totally. It is that Iraq posed no direct, immediate threat to Britain; and that Iraq's WMD, even on our own case, was not serious enough to warrant war, certainly without a specific UN resolution mandating 30 military action. And they argue: Saddam could, in any event, be contained.

In other words, they disagreed then and disagree now fundamentally with the characterisation of the threat. We were saying this is urgent; we have to act; the opponents of war 35 thought it wasn't. And I accept, incidentally, that however abhorrent and foul the regime and however relevant that was for the reasons I set out before the war, for example in Glasgow in February 2003, regime change alone could not be and was not our justification for war. Our primary purpose was to enforce UN resolutions over Iraq and WMD.

5 Of course the opponents are boosted by the fact that though we know Saddam had WMD; we haven't found the physical evidence of them in the 11 months since the war. But in fact, everyone thought he had them. That was the basis of UN Resolution 1441.

10 It's just worth pointing out that the search is being conducted in a country twice the land mass of the UK, which David Kay's interim report in October 2003 noted, contains 130 ammunition storage areas, some covering an area of 50 square miles, including some 600,000 tons of artillery shells, rockets and 15 other ordnance, of which only a small proportion have as yet been searched in the difficult security environment that exists. But the key point is that it is the threat that is the issue.

The characterisation of the threat is where the difference lies. Here is where I feel so passionately that we are in mortal dan- 20 ger of mistaking the nature of the new world in which we live. Everything about our world is changing: its economy, its technology, its culture, its way of living. If the 20th century scripted our conventional way of thinking, the 21st century is unconventional in almost every respect.

25 This is true also of our security.

The threat we face is not conventional. It is a challenge of a different nature from anything the world has faced before. It is to the world's security, what globalisation is to the world's economy.

30 It was defined not by Iraq but by September 11th. September 11th did not create the threat Saddam posed. But it altered crucially the balance of risk as to whether to deal with it or simply carry on, however imperfectly, trying to contain it. [...]

September 11th was for me a revelation. What had seemed 35 inchoate came together. The point about September 11th was not its detailed planning; not its devilish execution; not even, simply, that it happened in America, on the streets of New York. All of this made it an astonishing, terrible and wicked tragedy, a barbaric murder of innocent people. But what gal- 40 vanised me was that it was a declaration of war by religious fanatics who were prepared to wage that war without limit. They killed 3000. But if they could have killed 30,000 or 300,000 they would have rejoiced in it. The purpose was to cause such hatred between Moslems and the West that a reli- 45 gious jihad became reality; and the world engulfed by it.

to boost to give extra power or strength to

interim valid for the moment, not final
ammunition the material fired from a weapon
ordnance military supplies and materials

revelation here: sudden recognition of a previously hidden or little known fact
inchoate (*fml*) just starting to develop, esp. ideas, plans, attitudes

to galvanise to shock or surprise sb to solve a problem, improve a situation, etc.

jihad a holy war fought by Muslims
to engulf to flow over completely, here: to affect deeply

When I spoke to the House of Commons on 14 September, 2001, I said:

"We know, that they [the terrorists] would, if they could, go further and use chemical, biological, or even nuclear weapons of mass destruction. We know, also, that there are groups of 5 people, occasionally states, who will trade the technology and capability of such weapons. It is time that this trade was exposed, disrupted, and stamped out. We have been warned by the events of 11 September, and we should act on the warning."

From September 11th on, I could see the threat plainly. Here 10 were terrorists prepared to bring about Armageddon. Here were states whose leadership cared for no-one but themselves; were often cruel and tyrannical towards their own people; and who saw WMD as a means of defending themselves against any attempt external or internal to remove 15 them and who, in their chaotic and corrupt state, were in any event porous and irresponsible with neither the will nor capability to prevent terrorists who also hated the West, from exploiting their chaos and corruption. […]

The global threat to our security was clear. So was our duty: 20 to act to eliminate it.

First we dealt with Al Qaida in Afghanistan, removing the Taliban that succoured them.

But then we had to confront the states with WMD. [...]

I have no doubt Iraq is better without Saddam; but no doubt 25 either, that as a result of his removal, the dangers of the threat we face will be diminished. That is not to say the terrorists won't redouble their efforts. They will. This war is not ended. It may only be at the end of its first phase. They are in Iraq, murdering innocent Iraqis who want to worship or join a 30 police force that upholds the law not a brutal dictatorship; they carry on killing in Afghanistan. They do it for a reason. The terrorists know that if Iraq and Afghanistan survive their assault, come through their travails, seize the opportunity the future offers, then those countries will stand not just as 35 nations liberated from oppression, but as a lesson to humankind everywhere and a profound antidote to the poison of religious extremism. That is precisely why the terrorists are trying to foment hatred and division in Iraq. They know full well, a stable democratic Iraq, under the sovereign rule of the 40 Iraqi people, is a mortal blow to their fanaticism.

That is why our duty is to rebuild Iraq and Afghanistan as stable and democratic nations.

Here is the irony. For all the fighting, this threat cannot be defeated by security means alone. Taking strong action is a 45

Armageddon according to the Bible, the final terrible battle between the forces of good and evil that will destroy the world

porous here: allowing people to pass in and out freely, not secure

to succour (fml) to help

travail here: pain and suffering

antidote a substance that counteracts the effects of a poison
to foment (fml) to cause trouble and make people start fighting each other or the government [= stir up]

necessary but insufficient condition for defeating. Its final defeat is only assured by the triumph of the values of the human spirit.

Which brings me to the final point. It may well be that under
5 international law as presently constituted, a regime can systematically brutalise and oppress its people and there is nothing anyone can do, when dialogue, diplomacy and even sanctions fail, unless it comes within the definition of a humanitarian catastrophe (though the 300,000 remains in mass graves al-
10 ready found in Iraq might be thought by some to be something of a catastrophe). This may be the law, but should it be?

We know now, if we didn't before, that our own self-interest is ultimately bound up with the fate of other nations. The doctrine of international community is no longer a vision of
15 idealism. It is a practical recognition that just as within a country, citizens who are free, well-educated and prosperous tend to be responsible, to feel solidarity with a society in which they have a stake; so do nations that are free, demo- **stake** personal interest or share cratic and benefiting from economic progress, tend to be sta- in sth
20 ble and solid partners in the advance of humankind. The best defence of our security lies in the spread of our values.

But we cannot advance these values except within a framework that recognises their universality. If it is a global threat, **universality** truth or suitability it needs a global response, based on global rules. in every situation
25 The essence of a community is common rights and responsibilities. We have obligations in relation to each other. If we are threatened, we have a right to act. And we do not accept in a community that others have a right to oppress and brutalise their people. We value the freedom and dignity of the
30 human race and each individual in it.

Containment will not work in the face of the global threat **to proliferate** to increase that confronts us. The terrorists have no intention of being quickly and spread to many contained. The states that proliferate or acquire WMD illegally different places are doing so precisely to avoid containment. Emphatically I
35 am not saying that every situation leads to military action. But we surely have a duty and a right to prevent the threat materialising; and we surely have a responsibility to act when a nation's people are subjected to a regime such as Saddam's. Otherwise, we are powerless to fight the aggression and injus-
40 tice which over time puts at risk our security and way of life.

Which brings us to how you make the rules and how you decide what is right or wrong in enforcing them. The UN Universal Declaration on Human Rights is a fine document. But it is strange the United Nations is so reluctant to enforce
45 them. [...]

Declaration on Human Rights an official statement drafted by the UN in 1948 which says all people in the world should have access to basic human rights, such as the right to express their beliefs without being punished and the right to be treated fairly and according to the law

reluctant slow and unwilling **to enforce** to make people obey a rule or law

George W. Bush Jr.: **The world is engaged in a great ideological struggle (2006)**

President Bush addressed the United Nations General Assembly on September 19, 2006, one week after the fifth anniversary of the terrorist attacks on the World Trade Center to express his hopes for a better future.

United Nations (UN) an international organization that tries to find peaceful solutions to world problems

Mr. Secretary General, Madam President, distinguished delegates, and ladies and gentlemen: I want to thank you for the privilege of speaking to this General Assembly.

Last week, America and the world marked the fifth anniversary of the attacks that filled another September morning 5 with death and suffering. On that terrible day, extremists killed nearly 3,000 innocent people, including citizens of

chamber a large room in a public building used for important meetings

dozens of nations represented right here in this chamber. Since then, the enemies of humanity have continued their campaign of murder. Al Qaeda and those inspired by its ex- 10 tremist ideology have attacked more than two dozen nations.

deliberate intended or planned

And recently a different group of extremists deliberately provoked a terrible conflict in Lebanon. At the start of the 21st century, it is clear that the world is engaged in a great ideological struggle, between extremists who use terror as a weap- 15 on to create fear, and moderate people who work for peace.

Five years ago, I stood at this podium and called on the community of nations to defend civilization and build a more hopeful future. This is still the great challenge of our time; it is the calling of our generation. This morning, I want to speak 20 about the more hopeful world that is within our reach, a world beyond terror, where ordinary men and women are free to determine their own destiny, where the voices of mod-

to marginalize to make a person or a group of people unimportant and powerless

eration are empowered, and where the extremists are marginalized by the peaceful majority. This world can be ours if we 25 seek it and if we work together.

Universal Declaration of Human Rights an official statement drafted by the UN in 1948 which says all people in the world should have access to human rights, such as the right to express their beliefs without being punished and the right to be treated fairly and according to the law

The principles of this world beyond terror can be found in the very first sentence of the Universal Declaration of Human Rights. This document declares that the "equal and inalienable rights of all members of the human family is the 30 foundation of freedom and justice and peace in the world." [...]

Every civilized nation, including those in the Muslim world, must support those in the region who are offering a more hopeful alternative. We know that when people have a voice 35

inalienable (*fml*) that cannot be taken away

in their future, they are less likely to blow themselves up in

suicide attacks. We know that when leaders are accountable to their people, they are more likely to seek national greatness in the achievements of their citizens, rather than in terror and conquest. So we must stand with democratic leaders
5 and moderate reformers across the broader Middle East. We must give them voice to the hopes of decent men and women who want for their children the same things we want for ours. We must seek stability through a free and just Middle East where the extremists are marginalized by millions of
10 citizens in control of their own destinies.

Today, I'd like to speak directly to the people across the broader Middle East: My country desires peace. Extremists in your midst spread propaganda claiming that the West is engaged in a war against Islam. This propaganda is false, and its
15 purpose is to confuse you and justify acts of terror. We respect Islam, but we will protect our people from those who pervert Islam to sow death and destruction. Our goal is to help you build a more tolerant and hopeful society that honors people of all faiths and promote the peace.

20 To the people of Iraq: Nearly 12 million of you braved the car bombers and assassins last December to vote in free elections. The world saw you hold up purple ink-stained fingers, and your courage filled us with admiration. You've stood firm in the face of horrendous acts of terror and sectarian violence –
25 and we will not abandon you in your struggle to build a free nation. America and our coalition partners will continue to stand with the democratic government you elected. We will continue to help you secure the international assistance and investment you need to create jobs and opportunity, working
30 with the United Nations and through the International Compact with Iraq endorsed here in New York yesterday. We will continue to train those of you who stepped forward to fight the enemies of freedom. We will not yield the future of your country to terrorists and extremists. In return, your leaders
35 must rise to the challenges your country is facing, and make difficult choices to bring security and prosperity. Working together, we will help your democracy succeed, so it can become a beacon of hope for millions in the Muslim world.

To the people of Afghanistan: Together, we overthrew the
40 Taliban regime that brought misery into your lives and harbored terrorists who brought death to the citizens of many nations. Since then, we have watched you choose your leaders in free elections and build a democratic government. You can be proud of these achievements. We respect your courage,
45 and your determination to live in peace and freedom. We will

decent following moral standards that are acceptable to society

to sow to plant a seed; here: to spread

to brave sth *etwas die Stirn bieten*

sectarian violence fighting caused by disagreement between different religious groups

compact (*fml*) here: an agreement between countries or people
to endorse to express formal support or approval for sb or sth
to yield to give up

beacon a guiding light

Taliban a Muslim group which controlled most of Afghanistan from 1997 to 2001. The Taliban followed the laws of Islam very strictly.

NATO (North Atlantic Treaty Organization) a group of countries, including the US and several European countries, which give military help to each other

Hezbollah, also Hizbollah a military group of Shiite Muslims that supports Iran

resolution a formal decision or statement agreed on by a group of people, esp. after a vote

pluralism the belief that different religious, racial and political groups can co-exist peacefully

Hamas an organization of Islamic fundamentalists in Palestine

continue to stand with you to defend your democratic gains. Today forces from more than 40 countries, including members of the NATO Alliance, are bravely serving side-by-side with you against the extremists who want to bring down the free government you've established. We'll help you defeat ₅ these enemies and build a free Afghanistan that will never again oppress you, or be a safe haven for terrorists.

To the people of Lebanon: Last year, you inspired the world when you came out into the streets to demand your independence from Syrian dominance. You drove Syrian forces ₁₀ from your country and you re-established democracy. Since then, you have been tested by the fighting that began with Hezbollah's unprovoked attacks on Israel. Many of you have seen your homes and communities caught in crossfire. We see your suffering, and the world is helping you to rebuild your ₁₅ country, and helping you deal with the armed extremists who are undermining your democracy by acting as a state within a state. The United Nations has passed a good resolution that has authorized an international force, led by France and Italy, to help you restore Lebanese sovereignty over Lebanese soil. ₂₀ For many years, Lebanon was a model of democracy and pluralism and openness in the region – and it will be again.

To the people of Iran: The United States respects you; we respect your country. We admire your rich history, your vibrant culture, and your many contributions to civilization. You de- ₂₅ serve an opportunity to determine your own future, an economy that rewards your intelligence and your talents, and a society that allows you to fulfill your tremendous potential. The greatest obstacle to this future is that your rulers have chosen to deny you liberty and to use your nation's resources ₃₀ to fund terrorism, and fuel extremism, and pursue nuclear weapons. The United Nations has passed a clear resolution requiring that the regime in Tehran meet its international obligations.

Iran must abandon its nuclear weapons ambitions. Despite ₃₅ what the regime tells you, we have no objection to Iran's pursuit of a truly peaceful nuclear power program. We're working toward a diplomatic solution to this crisis. And as we do, we look to the day when you can live in freedom – and America and Iran can be good friends and close partners in ₄₀ the cause of peace.

To the people of Syria: Your land is home to a great people with a proud tradition of learning and commerce. Today your rulers have allowed your country to become a crossroad for terrorism. In your midst, Hamas and Hezbollah are working ₄₅

to destabilize the region, and your government is turning your country into a tool of Iran. This is increasing your country's isolation from the world. Your government must choose a better way forward by ending its support for terror, and liv-
5 ing in peace with your neighbors, and opening the way to a better life for you and your families. [...]

Freedom, by its nature, cannot be imposed – it must be chosen. From Beirut to Baghdad, people are making the choice for freedom. And the nations gathered in this chamber must
10 make a choice, as well: Will we support the moderates and reformers who are working for change across the Middle East – or will we yield the future to the terrorists and extremists? America has made its choice: We will stand with the moderates and reformers.

15 Recently a courageous group of Arab and Muslim intellectuals wrote me a letter. In it, they said this: "The shore of reform is the only one on which any lights appear, even though the journey demands courage and patience and perseverance." The United Nations was created to make that journey possi-
20 ble. Together we must support the dreams of good and decent people who are working to transform a troubled region – and by doing so, we will advance the high ideals on which this institution was founded.

Thank you for your time. God bless.

to impose to force sb to accept sth they don't want

perseverance *Ausdauer*

Global warming

George W. Bush Jr.: Clear skies and global climate change initiatives (2002)

Faced with mounting evidence of a global climate change, government leaders have been forced to react to this situation and to propose various steps for meeting the future challenges. Among them is President George W. Bush, who on 14 February 2002 announced a new approach to the challenge of global climate change. Nevertheless, he was met with criticism from other countries for not having ratified the Kyoto protocol. According to the White House, the new suggested approach is designed to harness the power of markets and technological innovation. The President's announcement included a proposal to cut power plant emissions, called the *Clear Skies Initiative*, as well as other initiatives designed to reduce greenhouse gas intensity, spur investments in renewable energy, and stimulate the development of technologies to combat global climate change.

Thank you very much for that warm welcome. It's an honor to join you all today to talk about our environment and about the prospect of dramatic progress to improve it.

Today, I'm announcing a new environmental approach that will clean our skies, bring greater health to our citizens and 5 encourage environmentally responsible development in America and around the world. [...]

America and the world share this common goal: we must foster economic growth in ways that protect our environment. We must encourage growth that will provide a better 10 life for citizens, while protecting the land, the water, and the air that sustain life.

to foster to help sb or sth to develop over a period of time

In pursuit of this goal, my government has set two priorities: we must clean our air, and we must address the issue of global climate change. We must also act in a serious and responsible 15 way, given the scientific uncertainties. While these uncertainties remain, we can begin now to address the human factors that contribute to climate change. Wise action now is an insurance policy against future risks.

I have been working with my Cabinet to meet these chal- 20 lenges with forward and creative thinking. I said, if need be, let's challenge the status quo. But let's always remember, let's do what is in the interest of the American people.

Today, I'm confident that the environmental path that I announce will benefit the entire world. This new approach is 25 based on this common-sense idea: that economic growth is key to environmental progress, because it is growth that provides the resources for investment in clean technologies.

to harness sth to control and use the natural force or power of sth
entrepreneur sb who starts or runs a successful business, often one involving financial risks

This new approach will harness the power of markets, the creativity of entrepreneurs, and draw upon the best scientific 30 research. And it will make possible a new partnership with the developing world to meet our common environmental and economic goals.

We will apply this approach first to the challenge of cleaning the air that Americans breathe. Today, I call for new Clean 35 Skies legislation that sets tough new standards to dramatically reduce the three most significant forms of pollution

from power plants, sulfur dioxide, nitrogen oxides and mercury.

mercury *Quecksilber*

We will cut sulfur dioxide emissions by 73 percent from current levels. We will cut nitrogen oxide emissions by 67 per-
5 cent. And, for the first time ever, we will cap emissions of
mercury, cutting them by 69 percent. These cuts will be completed over two measured phases, with one set of emission
limits for 2010 and for the other for 2018.

This legislation will constitute the most significant step
10 America has ever taken – has ever taken – to cut power plant
emissions that contribute to urban smog, acid rain and nu-
merous health problems for our citizens.

The term **acid rain** is
commonly used to mean the
deposition of acidic
components in rain, snow,
dew, or dry particles. Acid
rain occurs when sulfur
dioxide and nitrogen oxides
are emitted into the
atmosphere, undergo
chemical transformations
and are absorbed by water
droplets in clouds.

Clean Skies legislation will not only protect our environment, it will prolong the lives of thousands of Americans
15 with asthma and other respiratory illnesses, as well as with
those with heart disease. And it will reduce the risk to children exposed to mercury during a mother's pregnancy.

The Clean Skies legislation will reach our ambitious air quality goals through a market-based cap-and-trade approach
20 that rewards innovation, reduces cost and guarantees results.
Instead of the government telling utilities where and how to
cut pollution, we will tell them when and how much to cut.
We will give them a firm deadline and let them find the most
innovative ways to meet it.

Cap-and-trade systems
draw on the power of the
marketplace to reduce
emissions in a cost-effective
and flexible manner. In
practice, cap-and-trade
systems create a financial
incentive for emission
reductions by assigning a
cost to polluting.

25 We will do this by requiring each facility to have a permit for
each ton of pollution it emits. By making the permits trade-
able, this system makes it financially worthwhile for companies to pollute less, giving them an incentive to make early
and cost effective reductions.

utility a service such as gas or
electricity provided for people to
use

30 This approach enjoys widespread support, with both Democrats and Republicans, because we know it works. You see,
since 1995 we have used a cap-and-trade program for sulfur
dioxide pollution. It has cut more air pollution, this system
has reduced more air pollution in the last decade than all
35 other programs under the 1990 Clean Air Act combined. And
by even more than the law required. Compliance has been
virtually 100 percent. It takes only a handful of employees to
administer this program. And no one had to enter a court-
room to make sure the reductions happened.

The 1990 **Clean Air Act** is a
federal law covering the
entire country. Under this
law, the Environmental
Protection Agency sets limits
on how much of a pollutant
can be in the air anywhere in
the United States. This
ensures that all Americans
have the same basic health
and environmental
protections.

40 Because the system gives businesses an incentive to create
and install innovative technologies, these reductions have
cost about 80 percent less than expected. It helps to keep
energy prices affordable for our consumers. And we made
this progress during a decade when our economy, and our
45 demand for energy, was growing.

compliance the obeying of a
rule, agreement, or demand

maze here: a complicated and confusing arrangement
litigation the process of taking claims to a court of law

Over a decade ago, most countries joined the **United Nations Framework Convention** on Climate Change to begin to consider what can be done to reduce global warming and to cope with whatever temperature increases are inevitable.

The Clean Skies legislation I propose is structured on this approach because it works. It will replace a confusing, ineffective maze of regulations for power plants that has created an endless cycle of litigation. Today, hundreds of millions of dollars are spent on lawyers, rather than on environmental 5 protection. The result is painfully slow, uncertain and expensive programs on clean air.

Instead, Clean Skies legislation will put less money into paying lawyers and regulators, and money directly into programs to reduce pollution, to meet our national goal. This approach, 10 I'm absolutely confident, will bring better and faster results in cleaning up our air.

Now, global climate change presents a different set of challenges and requires a different strategy. The science is more complex, the answers are less certain, and the technology is 15 less developed. So we need a flexible approach that can adjust to new information and new technology.

I reaffirm America's commitment to the United Nations Framework Convention and its central goal, to stabilize atmospheric greenhouse gas concentrations at a level that will 20 prevent dangerous human interference with the climate. Our immediate goal is to reduce America's greenhouse gas emissions relative to the size of our economy.

My administration is committed to cutting our nation's greenhouse gas intensity – how much we emit per unit of 25 economic activity – by 18 percent over the next 10 years. This will set America on a path to slow the growth of our greenhouse gas emissions and, as science justifies, to stop and then reverse the growth of emissions.

This is the common sense way to measure progress. Our na- 30 tion must have economic growth – growth to create opportunity; growth to create a higher quality of life for our citizens. Growth is also what pays for investments in clean technologies, increased conservation, and energy efficiency. Meeting our commitment to reduce our greenhouse gas intensity by 35 18 percent by the year 2012 will prevent over 500 million metric tons of greenhouse gases from going into the atmosphere over the course of the decade. And that is the equivalent of taking 70 million cars off the road.

To achieve this goal, our nation must move forward on many 40 fronts, looking at every sector of our economy. We will challenge American businesses to further reduce emissions. Already, agreements with the semiconductor and aluminum industries and others have dramatically cut emissions of some of the most potent greenhouse gases. We will build on 45

these successes with new agreements and greater reductions.
Our government will also move forward immediately to create world-class standards for measuring and registering emission reductions. And we will give transferable credits to com-
5 panies that can show real emission reductions.
We will promote renewable energy production and clean coal
technology, as well as nuclear power, which produces no
greenhouse gas emissions. And we will work to safely improve fuel economy for our cars and our trucks.
10 Overall, my budget devotes $4.5 billion to addressing climate
change – more than any other nation's commitment in the
entire world. This is an increase of more than $700 million
over last year's budget. Our nation will continue to lead the
world in basic climate and science research to address gaps in
15 our knowledge that are important to decision makers.
When we make decisions, we want to make sure we do so on
sound science; not what sounds good, but what is real. And
the United States leads the world in providing that kind of
research. We'll devote $588 million towards the research and
20 development of energy conservation technologies. We must
and we will conserve more in the United States. And we will
spend $408 million toward research and development on re-
newables, on renewable energy.
This funding includes $150 million for an initiative that
25 Spencer Abraham laid out the other day, $150 million for the
Freedom Car Initiative, which will advance the prospect of
breakthrough zero-emission fuel cell technologies.
My comprehensive energy plan, the first energy plan that
any administration has put out in a long period of time, pro-
30 vides $4.6 billion over the next five years in clean energy tax
incentives to encourage purchases of hybrid and fuel cell ve-
hicles, to promote residential solar energy, and to reward investments in wind, solar and biomass energy production.
And we will look for ways to increase the amount of carbon
35 stored by America's farms and forests through a strong conservation title in the farm bill. I have asked Secretary Vene-
man to recommend new targeted incentives for landowners
to increase carbon storage.
By doing all these things, by giving companies incentives to
40 cut emissions, by diversifying our energy supply to include
cleaner fuels, by increasing conservation, by increasing research and development and tax incentives for energy efficiency and clean technologies, and by increasing carbon
storage, I am absolutely confident that America will reach
45 the goal that I have set.

In January 2002, the
FreedomCAR (Cooperative
Automotive Research)
program was announced to
fund research into hydrogen
fuel cells for cars. The
program is intended to
reduce vehicle emissions of
greenhouse gases and other
pollutants and end the
United States' dependence
on petroleum.

If, however, by 2012, our progress is not sufficient and sound science justifies further action, the United States will respond with additional measures that may include broad-based market programs as well as additional incentives and voluntary measures designed to accelerate technology development 5 and deployment.

Addressing global climate change will require a sustained effort over many generations. My approach recognizes that economic growth is the solution, not the problem. Because a nation that grows its economy is a nation that can afford 10 investments and new technologies.

The approach taken under the Kyoto protocol would have required the United States to make deep and immediate cuts in our economy to meet an arbitrary target. It would have cost our economy up to $400 billion and we would have lost 15 4.9 million jobs.

As President of the United States, charged with safeguarding the welfare of the American people and American workers, I will not commit our nation to an unsound international treaty that will throw millions of our citizens out of work. 20 Yet, we recognize our international responsibilities. So in addition to acting here at home, the United States will actively help developing nations grow along a more efficient, more environmentally responsible path.

[…] When I see what Americans have done, I know what we 25 can do. We can tap the power of economic growth to further protect our environment for generations that follow. And that's what we're going to do.

Thank you. (Applause.)

deployment the use of sth for a particular purpose, esp. ideas, arguments, etc.

arbitrary decided or arranged without any reason or plan, often unfairly

to safeguard to protect sth from harm or damage

to tap here: to make use of

Kofi Annan: Address to the climate change conference in Nairobi (2006)

Kenya successfully hosted the second meeting of the Parties to the Kyoto Protocol (COP/MOP 2), in conjunction with the twelfth session of the Conference of the Parties to the Climate Change Convention (COP 12), in Nairobi from 6 to 17 November, 2006. The Conference was attended by 6,000 participants from 180 countries, including the United Nations Secretary-General, Kofi Annan. The "Spirit of Nairobi" prevailed as the

United Nations Climate Change Conference successfully concluded with decisions to support developing countries. Kofi Annan made a clear statement in favour of meeting the challenges of global warming and climate change.

I thank the Government and people of Kenya for hosting this international conference. You have warmly welcomed thousands of people into your midst, and created excellent conditions for the crucially important work on our agenda. Thank
5 you for yet another strong show of support for the United Nations.

All of us in this hall are devoted to the betterment of the human condition. All of us want to see a day when everyone, not just a fortunate few, can live in dignity and look to the
10 future with hope. All of us want to create a world of harmony among human beings, and between them and the natural environment on which life depends.

That vision, which has always faced long odds, is now being placed in deeper jeopardy by climate change. Even the gains
15 registered in recent years risk being undone.

Climate change is not just an environmental issue, as too many people still believe. It is an all-encompassing threat.

It is a threat to health, since a warmer world is one in which infectious diseases such as malaria and yellow fever will
20 spread further and faster.

It could imperil the world's food supply, as rising temperatures and prolonged drought render fertile areas unfit for grazing or crops.

It could endanger the very ground on which nearly half the
25 world's population live – coastal cities such as Lagos or Cape Town, which face inundation from sea levels rising as a result of melting icecaps and glaciers.

All this and more lies ahead. Billion-dollar weather-related calamities. The destruction of vital ecosystems such as forests
30 and coral reefs. Water supplies disappearing or tainted by saltwater intrusion.

Climate change is also a threat to peace and security. Changing patterns of rainfall, for example, can heighten competition for resources, setting in motion potentially destabilizing
35 tensions and migrations, especially in fragile States or volatile regions. There is evidence that some of this is already occurring; more could well be in the offing.

This is not science fiction. These are plausible scenarios, based on clear and rigorous scientific modelling. A few die-
40 hard sceptics continue to deny "global warming" is taking

crucial sth extremely important, because everything else depends on it

long odds high numbers showing a high risk of losing
jeopardy danger

all-encompassing covering everything

to imperil to put sth or sb in danger
drought a long period of dry weather when there is not enough water for plants and animals to survive

inundation (*fml*) flooding

calamity a terrible event that causes a lot of damage or suffering
to taint to damage sth by adding an unwanted substance to it

volatile likely to change suddenly and without warning

to be in the offing to be likely to happen soon
diehard sb who opposes change and refuses to accept new ideas

to sow doubt make sb feel uncertain about sth

perilous very dangerous

shift here: a change in the way people think about sth

disruption here: disorder
on a par with as bad as

The **Great Depression** was a time of economic downturn, which started after the stock market crash on October 29, 1929, known as Black Tuesday.

woeful very bad or serious
to spur to encourage sb or sth

surging suddenly increasing
constraint-based based on sth that limits your freedom

sustainable able to continue without causing lasting damage to the environment
to stifle here: to hold back or suppress
aspiration a strong desire to have or achieve sth

livelihood the way you earn money in order to live
sustenance food that people or animals need in order to live

place and try to sow doubt. They should be seen for what they are: out of step, out of arguments and out of time. In fact, the scientific consensus is becoming not only more complete, but also more alarming. Many scientists long known for their caution are now saying that global warming 5 trends are perilously close to a point of no return.

A similar shift may also be taking place among economists. Earlier this month, a study by the former chief economist of the World Bank, Sir Nicholas Stern of the United Kingdom, called climate change "the greatest and widest-ranging mar- 10 ket failure ever seen". He warned that climate change could shrink the global economy by 20 per cent, and cause economic and social disruption on a par with the two World Wars and the Great Depression.

The good news is that there is much we can do in response. 15 We have started using fossil fuels more cleanly and efficiently. Renewable energy is increasingly available at competitive prices. With more research and development – current levels are woefully, dangerously low – we could be much farther along. 20

Spurred by the Kyoto Protocol, international carbon finance flows to developing countries could reach $100 billion per year. Markets for low-carbon energy products are expected to grow dramatically. But we need more "green" approaches to meet surging energy demand. And we need to put the right 25 incentives in place to complement the constraint-based efforts that have prevailed to date.

The climate challenge offers real opportunities to advance development and place our societies on a more sustainable path. Low emissions need not mean low growth, or stifling a 30 country's development aspirations. So let there be no more denial. Let no one say we cannot afford to act. It is increasingly clear that it will cost far less to cut emissions now than to deal with the consequences later. And let there be no more talk of waiting until we know more. We know already that an 35 economy based on high emissions is an uncontrolled experiment on the global climate.

But even as we seek to cut emissions, we must at the same time do far more to adapt to global warming and its effects. The impact of climate change will fall disproportionately on 40 the world's poorest countries, many of them here in Africa. Poor people already live on the front lines of pollution, disaster and the degradation of resources and land. Their livelihoods and sustenance depend directly on agriculture, forestry and fisheries. Think, for example, of the women and 45

girls forced to forage for fuel and water in the absence of basic energy services. Or of the innumerable African communities that have suffered climate-related disasters in recent years. The floods of Mozambique, the droughts in the Sahel and
5 here in Kenya, are fresh in our memories. For them, adaptation is a matter of sheer survival. We must make it a higher priority to integrate the risks posed by climate change into strategies and programmes aimed at achieving the Millennium Development Goals.
10 The message is clear. Global climate change must take its place alongside those threats – conflict, poverty, the proliferation of deadly weapons – that have traditionally monopolized first-order political attention. And the United Nations offers the tools the world needs to respond.
15 Regional and national initiatives have their value. But the UN Framework Convention is the forum in which a truly global response is being formulated. The Kyoto Protocol is now fully operational, and its Clean Development Mechanism has become a multibillion-dollar source of funding for
20 sustainable development.
This mechanism is an outstanding example of a UN-led partnership linking government action to the private sector in the developing world. I am pleased to announce that six UN agencies have launched, at this conference, the "Nairobi
25 Framework", a plan to support developing countries, especially in Africa, to participate in the Clean Development Mechanism. I encourage donor countries to help make these efforts a success. I am also pleased to note that today, UNDP and UNEP are embarking on an initiative to help developing
30 countries, again including in Africa, to factor climate change into national development plans – so-called "climate proofing" in areas such as infrastructure.
UN agencies will continue to bring their expertise to bear. But the primary responsibility for action rests with indivi-
35 dual States – and for now, that means those that have been largely responsible for the accumulation of carbon dioxide in the atmosphere. They must do much more to bring their emissions down. While the Kyoto Protocol is a crucial step forward, that step is far too small. And as we consider how to
40 go further still, there remains a frightening lack of leadership.
In developing countries, meanwhile, emissions cannot continue to grow uncontrolled. Many of them have taken impressive action on climate change. Rapidly growing econ-
45 omies, like China, have been increasingly successful in

to forage to search for food or other supplies

The eight **Millennium Development Goals** range from halving extreme poverty to halting the spread of HIV/AIDS and providing universal primary education, all by the target date of 2015.

proliferation increase

Over a decade ago, most countries joined the **United Nations Framework Convention** on Climate Change to begin to consider what can be done to reduce global warming.

The **Kyoto Protocol** to the United Nations Framework Convention on Climate Change is an amendment to the international treaty on climate, assigning mandatory emission limitations for the reduction of greenhouse gas emissions to the signatory nations.

UNDP is the UN's global development network, an organization advocating change and connecting countries to knowledge, experience and resources to help people build a better life.

UNEP, established in 1972, is the voice for the environment within the United Nations system. UNEP acts as a catalyst, advocate, educator and facilitator to promote the wise use and sustainable development of the global environment.

to factor to include sth in one's planning, etc.

to decouple to separate, disconnect

compelling powerful, difficult to resist

decoupling economic growth from energy use, thereby reducing the emission intensities of their economies. But more needs to be done.

Business, too, can do its part. Changes in corporate behaviour, and in the way private investment is directed, will prove 5 at least as significant in winning the climate battle as direct Government action.

And individuals too have roles to play. A single energy-efficient light bulb placed in a kitchen socket may not seem like much; but multiplied by millions, the savings are impressive. 10 Voting power could be similarly compelling, if people were to make action on climate change more of an election issue than it is today and individuals, through their purchasing choices, can put pressure on corporations to go green.

There is still time for all our societies to change course. In- 15 stead of being economically defensive, let us start being more politically courageous. The Nairobi Conference must send a clear, credible signal that the world's political leaders take climate change seriously. The question is not whether climate change is happening or not, but whether, in the face of 20 this emergency, we ourselves can change fast enough.

Biographies

Rudy Giuliani (*1944) was born to a working class family of Italian immigrants in Brooklyn, New York. In 1993, his campaign focusing on quality of life, crime, business and education made him the 107th Mayor of the City of New York. In 1997 he was re-elected. As Mayor, Rudy Giuliani returned accountability to City government and improved the quality of life for all New Yorkers. Since leaving the office of Mayor, he has held various positions in the business world and is currently seeking the Republican nomination for president.

Osama Bin Laden (*1957) was born in Dschidda, Saudi Arabia and is best known as the mastermind behind the 11 September 2001 attacks on the World Trade Center in New York. The US government considers Osama bin Laden to be the most dangerous terrorist in the world.

Colin L. Powell (*1937) was a professional soldier for 35 years. In 2001, then-President-elect George W. Bush Jr. nominated General Colin L. Powell as US Secretary of State. The Senate easily approved the nomination, and General Powell became the first African American to hold the post. Some of his duties have included serving as the President's principal adviser on US foreign policy, conducting negotiations relating to US foreign affairs, and negotiating all treaties with foreign governments. He announced his resignation as Secretary of State in 2004 and President Bush nominated National Security Advisor Condoleezza Rice as Powell's successor.

Tony Blair (*1953): At just 30 years of age, Tony Blair won a seat in the 1983 General Election. In 1997, he led the Labour Party to landslide victory in the General Election after 18 years in Opposition. This meant that, at the age of 43, Tony Blair became one of the youngest Prime Ministers in the history of Great Britain. He stepped back from office in June 2007.

George W. Bush Jr. (*1946) is the 43rd President of the United States and the eldest son of former US President, George H.W. Bush. Having served previously as the 47th Governor of Texas from 1995 to 2000, Bush was first elected president in a close and controversial contest in the 2000 presidential election. In

October 2001, after the September 11th attacks, Bush declared a "Global War on Terrorism", authorizing first military attacks on Afghanistan and later the invasion of Iraq. Positioning himself as a war president in the midst of the Iraq war, he was able to gain re-election in 2004. However, since then, his approval ratings have declined considerably, due in large part, to his uncompromising stance on Iraq and refusal to accept the proposals for combating global climate change outlined in the Kyoto Protocol.

Kofi Atta Annan (*1938): Born in Ghana, Annan studied at the University of Science and Technology in Kumasi and in the United States. He undertook graduate studies in Economics at the Institut Universitaire des Hautes Etudes Internationales in Geneva. As a 1971–1972 Sloan Fellow at the Massachusetts Institute of Technology, Annan received a Master of Science degree in Management. At UN Headquarters in New York, he held senior positions in a diverse range of areas before serving as Secretary General of the UN from 1997 until 2006. As Secretary General, Mr. Annan gave priority to revitalizing the UN through a comprehensive programme of reform; strengthening the Organization's traditional work in the areas of development and the maintenance of international peace and security; advocating human rights, especially the rule of law and the universal values of equality, tolerance and human dignity and restoring public confidence in the Organization by reaching out to new partners. In 2001, he was the co-recipient of the Nobel Peace Prize.

Developing skills

Parts of a speech

A speech usually has three main parts:
- Introduction (grab audience's attention, orients the listeners to the topic and prepares them for the speech)
- Main body (contains most of the information; each main point is clearly stated and supported by subordinate points)
- Conclusion (reviews the main points and provides closure by ending with a strong, final statement)

Types of speeches

- Inaugural speech/address
- State of the Union address
- Funeral oration
- Election speech
- Opening address
- Acceptance speech
- Closing argument in court
- Commemorative speech
- ...

Useful words and expressions

Attracting the audience's attention

The speaker	makes clear the purpose of his speech	by ...
	begins his speech with a quotation/anecdote ...	
	introduces his/her speech	by giving ...
	draws the audience's attention	to ...
	engages the audience	by ...

Persuasion

The speaker	tries to impress the audience	by …
	tries to make the audience adopt his/her view	
	expands on the point	that …
	bases his/her arguments on statements	that …
	uses short sentences	to …
	backs up his/her ideas with facts/statistics/…	
	includes personal experiences ("I", "we") in order to bond with the audience	
	uses rhetorical devices to convince the audience	
	tries to win the audience over to his/her side	
	appeals to the audience's emotions	
	asserts …	
	contends …	
	maintains …	
	argues …	
	points out …	

The speaker's	objective is to convince the audience	of …
	argumentation is based on	
	references	to …

Ending the speech

The speaker	sums up his/her main ideas/arguments …
	mentions a possible future outlook
	asks the audience to support his/her view …
	calls his/her audience to action

Rhetorical devices

Rhetorical device	Example	Explanation
Alliteration	"Fourscore and seven years ago our fathers brought forth on this continent a new nation ..." (A. Lincoln, *Gettysburg address*)	Repetition of the same sound beginning several words in sequence
Anaphora	"We have before us an ordeal of the most grievous kind. We have before us many, many long months of struggle and suffering." (W. Churchill, *Blood, toil, tears and sweat*)	Repetition of a word or phrase at the beginning of successive phrases, clauses or lines
Antithesis	Brutus: "Not that I loved Caesar less, but that I loved Rome more." (W. Shakespeare, *Julius Caesar*)	Opposition, or contrast of ideas or words in a balanced or parallel construction
Asyndeton	"But, in a larger sense, we cannot dedicate, we cannot consecrate, we cannot hallow this ground." (A. Lincoln, *Gettysburg address*)	Lack of conjunctions between coordinate phrases, clauses, or words
Climax	"It is a threat to health, since a warmer world is one in which infectious diseases such as malaria and yellow fever will spread further and faster. It could imperil the world's food supply as rising temperatures and prolonged drought render fertile areas unfit for grazing or crops. It could endanger the very ground on which nearly half the world's population live ..." (K. Annan, *Address to the climate change conference in Nairobi*)	Arrangement of words, phrases, or clauses in an order of ascending importance. Often the last emphatic word in one phrase or clause is repeated as the first emphatic word of the next.
Hyperbole	"Many will turn away – away from this man; for he is not a man but a demon, a monster, a subverter and an enemy of the black man – and we will smile." (Ossie Davis, *Our shining black prince*)	Exaggeration for emphasis or for rhetorical effect
Irony	"Yet Brutus says he was ambitious; And Brutus is an honourable man." (W. Shakespeare, *Julius Caesar*)	Expression of something which is contrary to the intended meaning; the words say one thing but the speaker means another.

Rhetorical device	Example	Explanation
Metaphor	"We have to build the noble mansion of free India where all her children may dwell." (J. Nehru, *Speech on the granting of Indian independence*)	Implied comparison achieved through a figurative use of words; the word is used not in its literal sense, but in one analogous to it.
Onomato-poeia	"He clattered and clanged as he washed the dishes."	Use of words to imitate natural sounds; accommodation of sound to sense
Parallelism	"On this day our first thoughts go to the architect of this freedom, the Father of our Nation, ... Our next thoughts must be of the unknown volunteers and soldiers ..." (J. Nehru, *Speech on the granting of Indian independence*)	Successive clauses or sentences are similarly structured. This similarity makes it easier for the reader/listener to concentrate on the message.
Personifi-cation	"Harlem has come to bid farewell to one of its brightest hopes." (Ossie Davis, *Our shining black prince*)	Attribution of personality to an impersonal thing
Repetition	"There are some who say that Communism is the wave of the future. Let them come to Berlin. And there are some who say in Europe and elsewhere we can work with the Communists. Let them com to Berlin." (J. F. Kennedy, *The Berlin speech*)	Words or phrases are repeated throughout the text to emphasize certain facts or ideas.
Rhetorical question	"Did this in Caesar seem ambitious?" (W. Shakespeare, *Julius Caesar*)	The author/speaker raises a question, but does not answer it directly as he/she sees the answer (usually yes or no) as obvious.
Simile	"Then there are high-profile examples of the absurd ... like radical clerics coming here to preach religious hate ..." (T. Blair, *Immigration and politics do not make easy bedfellows*)	An explicit comparison between two things using 'like' or 'as'.

Acknowledgements

Texts

William Shakespeare: Marc Antony's funeral oration. From: William Shakespeare, Julius Caesar, Harmondsworth, Penguin, 1967, III.2, ll. 63 – 163

Abraham Lincoln: Gettysburg address. From: www.yale.edu/lawweb/avalon/gettyb.htm

Winston Churchill: Blood, toil, tears and sweat. From: www.fiftiesweb.com/usa/winston-churchill-blood-toil.htm

John Fitzgerald Kennedy: The Berlin speech. From: www.americanrhetoric.com/speeches/jfkberliner.html

Hillary Rodham Clinton: America's best days are still ahead. From: www.clinton.senate.gov/news/statements/details.cfm? id=241057

George W. Bush: The United States must secure its borders. From: www.whitehouse.gov/news/releases/2006/05/20060515-8.html

Malcolm X: The ballot or the bullet. From: www.americanrhetoric.com/speeches/malcolmxballotorbullet.htm. © Estate of Malcolm X

Ossie Davis: Our shining black prince. From: www.hartford-hwp.com/archives/45a/071.html. Copyright © 1999 White Dragon Ventures

Robert F. Kennedy: I have some very sad news for all of you. From: www.americanrhetoric.com/speeches/rfkonmlkdeath.html

Bill Cosby: It's what you are not doing. From: www.americanrhetoric.com/speeches/billcosbypoundcakespeech.htm

Queen Elizabeth II: Annus horribilis. From: www.royal.gov.uk/output/Page4104.asp

Michael Portillo: The causes of defeat. From: www.michaelportillo.co.uk/speeches/speeches_pub/speech13p.htm

Tony Blair: We are the change-maker. From: www.labour.org.uk/index.php?id=news2005&ux_news%5Bid%5D=ac05tb&cHash=d8353c3d74

Arthur Scargill: Fight for the future. From: www.num.org.uk/?p=history&c=speeches&id=30

Margaret Thatcher: The strike is over. From: www.margaretthatcher.org/speeches/displaydocument.asp?docid=106000. Copyright © Margaret Thatcher Foundation 2007

Tony Benn: I cannot hand away powers lent to me. From: The Penguin Book of 20th Century Speeches, ed. by Brian MacArthur, London, Penguin, 1999, pp. 479 – 482

Douglas Alexander: Britain's place in today's European Union. From: www.fco.gov.uk/servlet/Front?pagename=OpenMarket/Xcelerate/ShowPage&c=Page&cid=1140686158923&print=true&a=KArticle&aid=1115140100509

Mahatma Gandhi: Quit India. From: www.famousquotes.me.uk/speeches/Mahatma_Gandhi/index.htm

Clement Attlee: The end of British rule in India. From: Hansard's Parliamentary Debates [House of Commons], 5th Series, Vol. 433, cols. 1395 – 1398

Winston Churchill: Britain's shameful flight from India. From: Hansard's Parliamentary Debates [House of Commons], 5th Series, Vol. 434, cols. 663 – 678

Jawaharlal Nehru: The granting of Indian independence. From: The Penguin Book of 20th Century Speeches, ed. by Brian MacArthur, London, Penguin, 1999, pp. 237 – 240

A. L. Geyer: A case for apartheid. From: Union of South Africa Government Information Pamphlet, New York, 1953. Reprinted in: Ruth E. Gordon and Clive Talbot (eds.): From Dias to Vorster. Source Material on South African History 1488–1975, Goodwood, S.A. Nasou, 1977, pp. 409–410

Harold Macmillan: The wind of change. From: The Penguin Book of 20th Century Speeches, ed. by Brian MacArthur, London, Penguin, 1999, pp. 286–289

Hendrik Verwoerd: Response to Harold Macmillan's speech. From: http://africanhistory.about.com/od/eraindependence/p/wind_of_change3.htm

Enoch Powell: River of blood. From: www.vdare.com/misc/powell_speech.htm

Tony Blair: Immigration and politics do not make easy bedfellows. From: www.number-10.gov.uk/output/page5708.asp

Rudy Giuliani: New York City was viciously attacked. From: www.american-rhethoric.com/speeches/rudygiuliani911unitednations.htm

Osama Bin Laden: Statement to the "infidel" nations. From: www.american-rhetoric.com/speeches/binladen10-07-01a.htm

Colin L. Powell: The United States is taking on the fight against terrorism. From: www.state.gov/secretary/former/powell/remarks/2001/6049.htm

Tony Blair: My divisive decision to go to war in Iraq. From: http://politics.guardian.co.uk/iraq/story/0.12956,1162991,00html. Guardian Unlimited © Guardian News and Media Limited 2007

George W. Bush: The world is engaged in a great ideological struggle. From: www.whitehouse.gov/news/releases/2006/09/20060919-4.html

George W. Bush: Clear skies and global climate change initiatives. From: www.whitehouse.gov/news/releases/2002/02/20020214-5html

Kofi Annan: Address to the climate change conference in Nairobi. From: www.ens-newswire.com/ens/nov2006/2006-11-15-insann.asp

Illustrations

p. 6/7: © picture-alliance/dpa (background); p. 6: © ullstein bild – Roger Viollet (Lincoln), © action press/PHOTOLINK (H. Clinton), © ullstein bild – AP (bin Laden), © ullstein bild – Lehnartz (Kennedy), © picture-alliance/dpa (Bush, Queen Elizabeth); p. 7: © dpa-Fotoreport/epa AFP Ray Abrams (Annan), picture-alliance/KPA/HIP/Ann Ronan Picture Library (Gandhi), © dpa (Churchill), © ullstein bild – KPA (Malcolm X), © ullstein – Boness/IPON (Blair), © vario-images/Ulrich Baumgarten (Thatcher); p. 17: S. F. James/Royal Studios, Wimborne Minster (GB) (Marc Antony), © ullstein bild – Roger Viollet (Lincoln); p. 18: © AP Photo; p. 41: © dpa-Fotoreport (Bush), © Cinetext (Davis); p. 42: © ullstein bild – KPA; p. 66: © ullstein bild – iT (Portillo, Scargill), © ullstein bild – KPA (Benn); p. 98: © ullstein bild – Karsh; p. 99: © akg-images (Nehru), © ullstein bild – iT (Macmillan), © ullstein bild – Camera Press Ltd. (Verwoerd), © ullstein bild – KPA (Powell); p. 125: © ullstein bild – AP (Guiliani), © ullstein bild – phalanx Fotoagentur (Powell)

Every effort has been made to supply complete copyright information for the texts and pictures included here. Should such entries be incomplete or contain errors, we request copyright owners to contact the publishers so that we can proceed with the necessary corrections.